Managing Staff in Early Y Settings

G000278416

This book draws on a wide range of management theory and shows its relevance and relationship to early years settings. Case studies are used to provide the starting-point for reflection, and throughout the chapters you are asked to consider the examples, stand back, interpret and audit your own actions in order to develop your management skills. This book will assist managers and prospective managers by providing them with the tools to facilitate staff training sessions or to conduct personal enquiry into the working of their own organisation.

Chapters cover leadership and management; teams and team building; staff motivation; managing change; selecting suitable staff and effective interviewing; staff assessment; projecting and maintaining a positive image for your school or nursery; and managing conflict and stress.

Adrian Smith is senior lecturer in the Management Department at Edge Hill University College, Ormskirk and **Ann Langston** is Early Years Adviser in a local authority.

Managing Staff in Early Years Settings

Adrian Smith and Ann Langston

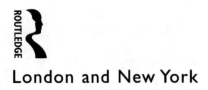

London and New York

First published 1999
by Routledge
11 New Fetter Lane, London EC4P 4EE

Simultaneously published in the USA and Canada
by Routledge
29 West 35th Street, New York, NY 10001

Typeset in Garamond by
J&L Composition Ltd, Filey, North Yorkshire
Printed and bound in Great Britain by
Creative Print and Design (Wales), Ebbw Vale

British Library Cataloguing in Publication Data
A catalogue record for this book is available
from the British Library

Library of Congress Cataloging in Publication Data
Smith, Adrian.
   Managing staff in early years settings/Adrian Smith and Ann
Langston.
     p.   cm.
   1. Child care workers – Training of.   2. Child care services –
Administration.   3. Early childhood education – Administration.
I. Langston, Ann. II. Title.
   HQ778.5.S63   1999
   362.7'068–dc21   98-40346
                                                             CIP

ISBN 0–415–17153–9

Contents

Figures

Tables

Introduction

Early years provision has never experienced such a high profile as it is currently enjoying, and as a result senior staff within those settings are under considerable pressure to manage children, staff, budgets, resources and parents with maximum efficiency. Fortunately, many senior staff are successful in doing all their tasks well without the benefit of appropriate training. Needless to say, we believe that this book contains much that will be of value to managers at all levels and phases within education and social services.

Many people who would never have described themselves as 'managers' find themselves having to make management decisions and frequently feel the lack of guidance and support. Similarly, those who are fortunate enough to receive management training frequently find it difficult to locate reading material aimed at settings they recognise, since many books on management have been related to business and enterprise cultures rather than to nurseries, crèches, playgroups or first schools. However, it must be stressed at the outset that this book is about *managing staff* and we hope it will prove useful for all managers in education, regardless of the phase in which they work.

We believe that there are still too few opportunities for management training and that current training programmes often fail to address the issues in sufficient depth. Furthermore, where staff development is provided, organisations tend to select specific curricular or establishment needs above the professional and personal requirements of individuals. Thus, for example, while staff may be supported in developing their expertise in Child Protection, or a curriculum area such as literacy, the courses that extend personal development are often squeezed out due to lack of funding or the low priority placed on them by services. While none of this is unexpected in today's climate of efficiency and cost-effectiveness, the training and development of staff can and should be viewed as an investment in the long-term future of all organisations.

In writing a book on management in early years settings we have been mindful of a number of things. First, we have endeavoured to contribute to a body of knowledge by drawing on management theory and showing its relevance and relationship to early years settings. Second, we have focused on a variety of ideas and theories rather than settling for the more limited and predictable ones. Third, we have attempted to provide a handbook that will assist managers and prospective managers by providing them with the tools to facilitate staff training sessions or to conduct personal enquiry into the working of their own organisation. Last, we have provided fertile ground for the student who will need to examine management issues in the course of either initial training or continuing professional development (CPD).

Management in the early years is, in many ways, no different from any other phase since it is about developing an organisation by identifying a vision, planning how that vision is to be realised, working towards achieving it and reviewing progress at points along the way. Over seventy years ago Henri Fayol, often considered to be the father of management theory, set out his principles of planning, organising, coordinating and controlling – many of which are still adhered to today and still apply to higher education, schools or nurseries. What is important is the emphasis we place on early years settings and their unique environments. Throughout the book we have endeavoured to highlight those areas that most affect staff and the way particular approaches can be used as a basis for solving or resolving management issues. Case studies are used to provide the starting point for reflection, and throughout the chapters you are asked to consider the examples, stand back, interpret and audit your own actions in order to develop your management skills. Every character and scenario is fictitious, but we believe, based on our experience of running courses for teachers and our work in a local education authority, nevertheless contains enough authenticity to provide a valid starting-point.

Such a developmental stance is adopted with no apology. We believe that everyone has the potential to be an effective manager. What is needed, in our view, is guidance and the opportunity to construct a framework in which to identify yourself and your own experiences. In order to do this we have provided examples, taken from a range of early years establishments, that highlight particular management issues early years professionals are likely to encounter in their daily work.

The locality in which you work may house any number of organisations whose purpose is to provide appropriate care and education for young children. It might seem, to the uninitiated, that this would exclude **schools**; however, this is not the case and we have included schools because they are familiar to us all and increasingly cater for children as young as 4 years old in reception classes. Schools also accommodate children in their nursery classes and occasionally host other organisations such as pre-school groups (formerly playgroups), toddler groups, Portage groups and so on. Within the school system but separate from it are a number of nursery schools, self sufficient, but funded by local education authorities.

Another large provider of early care and education are the **social services** which routinely provide day care for babies and young children in day nurseries, family centres and combined nursery centres. **Voluntary sector provision** includes a further range of establishments including pre-schools, nurseries, family centres and family support centres. Then there is the **private sector** which provides a range of facilities including full day care, nursery schools and crèches.

The organisation of the book

Our knowledge of the variety of audiences that may benefit from this book persuaded us to devise a text which could offer both theory and practice to managers. There are eleven chapters in all, each one addressing a specific issue that is examined in some depth. We have assumed that the reader has little or no knowledge of management theory and that her or his first need is for practical guidance in how to handle a particular task such as team building; at the same time we are aware that many who turn to this book will do so because they are practitioners studying the theory of management in an attempt to understand how the theory applies to their own 'unique' setting. Whichever group you are in we hope you will find something relevant to help make your task easier, whether that is to perfect your management skills, or to understand your own organisation in the light of the theory. If you are in the latter group you may also wish to read further – what we offer is only a taster on each topic and if you wish you can find much more information on any specific point from the further reading sections at the end of most chapters.

Chapter 1 focuses on leadership and management because we believe that it is upon the success of this cornerstone of any organisation that establishments will succeed or fail. In this chapter we examine leadership skills, management strategies and time management, and examples are provided of how practising managers can develop their performance in order to ensure firm leadership in an early years setting.

The focus moves in chapter 2 to working with others – a requirement for success in any establishment. The case study illustrates how working in groups is influenced by attitudes and behaviours of individuals; how teams can enhance their performance and how to identify potential problems with teams.

In chapter 3 the emphasis is upon team building, with a review of strategies for building a successful team and an examination of how to develop effective teams.

Maintaining the motivation of staff follows in chapter 4 and we encourage managers of people to consider how motivation and morale are linked, and offer ideas for managers to develop the motivation of their staff.

As we discussed earlier, change currently plays a major role in all early years settings and chapter 5 is focused on managing the challenge of change. This significant issue is considered in terms of the skills needed to manage change, providing guidelines for successful change and exploring how resistance to change can be overcome.

Chapter 6 provides an in-depth examination of the ways in which communication can either destroy or support effective working. It identifies examples of effective communication, besides examining barriers to communication.

The following three chapters review the ways in which staff selection and development should be determined in early years settings. In chapter 7 the focal point is selection procedures, while chapter 8 discusses strategies for effective interviewing. In chapter 9 the emphasis falls upon the role of management in staff development.

In the final chapters two difficult issues are addressed; marketing the school or nursery is dealt with in chapter 10, while managing conflict and stress is the subject of chapter 11.

Clearly there are no textbook answers available for managers seeking to resolve individual and organisational demands; indeed, most schools and centres run smoothly and operate effectively most of the time. However, that should not prevent managers from reflecting on activities and events to increase their self-confidence and prepare them for unforeseen circumstances. Through examination and discussion of the case studies we provide the manager with reflection points and activities intended to give her or him a helping hand to increase her or his own self-confidence and to make the task easier. Each reflection point should help you to think something through, but bear in mind that there may not necessarily be a 'right answer'.

From reflection we move to activity, where appropriate. Each activity provides clearly laid out tables, diagrams or charts to complete, so that the book will build into a working document that reflects your progress through the chapters. You do not need to follow each chapter slavishly however, and we recommend that you begin by selecting the issues most important to you before moving into other areas.

Finally, the book is not designed to be exclusive. We believe that an audience far wider than those in charge of others will benefit from participating in many of the tasks. Our view is that you are either a manager today, or the aspiring or reluctant one of tomorrow, forced to undertake some of the rapid decision making that characterises educational practice in the 1990s. We hope that in outlining some of the skills required you will develop the confidence to work effectively and achieve your potential. Our aims can be summarised thus:

- To encourage a creative approach to managerial problems through an understanding of theory and practice.
- To provide a source book for managers in early years settings in which they can identify elements of their own situations.
- To offer guidance and reflection for staff whose task is to manage change.
- To take a developmental view of change in early years education.

We hope that each chapter stands alone in addressing a specific topic but we are aware that managers frequently have to consider a range of issues and that some are interrelated. The way you use this book will depend upon your needs and purposes. We wish you success whether that be in managing effectively, leading management training sessions, developing your own skills in preparation for management or in studying management theories.

Having trawled through the theories, Ann has concluded that successful management depends largely upon being able to 'decentre' and see things from the perspective of another person – something we encourage in young children, but know takes time, practice and praise before it is perfected. Remember, we do not see things as *they* are, we see them as *we* are!

Acknowledgements

We are grateful to Sefton Metropolitan Authority for permission to reproduce examples from their personnel profiles in the Appendix to chapter 8. Figure 6.1 from Peel, M. (1995) *Improving Your Communication Skills*, London: Kogan Page, is reprinted by permission.

Chapter 1

Leadership and management

> This chapter focuses on: Leadership skills
> Management strategies
> Time management
>
> with examples of how you might improve your performance.

We introduce Gwen, a newly appointed head of a nursery school, who, though
a good practitioner, has had little training in the management of others. The
case study is designed to highlight some of the issues that professionals face in
a new climate of diverse demands and external pressures. Through an examination of Gwen's performance we will explore the differences between leaders
and managers and invite you to consider some of the skills you will need to
develop in order to manage others effectively. Each of the models discussed is
followed by a personal audit for you to complete and at the end of the chapter
you will find reference to further reading, should you wish to explore an area
in more depth.

Leadership and management complement each other. They both require the
ability to relate to people in a range of circumstances. Where they differ is with
regard to change. Managers cope with the complexities and results of change
while leaders inspire and initiate change. Both characteristics are important in
the context of change within education, particularly at the pre-school stage,
where the parent/client teacher/manager relationship is altering rapidly. In
order for early years establishments to achieve the high standards expected of
them, they must attract people who are capable of motivating others towards
attainable goals: in short, leaders who will inspire loyalty and act as a driving
force. The same person, however, needs to establish procedures for staff and
make a rational and balanced assessment of current situations; she or he needs
to be able to plan, to organise, to forecast and to control so that visions are

turned into reality. As well as being a leader and a manager, the same person needs to be an efficient administrator who checks the tasks, procedures and resources within the organisation. The sort of person who can successfully lead others has to combine all three elements — leader, manager, administrator — no mean feat, and a little like spinning plates! The leader initiates the ideas and puts them into practice. The manager keeps them going and organises their progress. The administrator makes sure that they are achievable. As you examine the case study, you will see that in Gwen's case, as for many people, there is a degree of overlap as she combines all three roles in her search for effectiveness.

[handwritten margin note: EY - 3 elements in one person]

Before beginning to read the chapter it would be useful to have a pencil and paper near you to complete the personal audit. We also suggest that you study the nursery layout (Figure 1.1) and staff list and backgrounds (Table 1.1).

Table 1.1 Details of staff

Staffing Role	Name/ Qualifications	Experience
Recently appointed head teacher	Gwen B.Ed. (Early years)	Two previous posts as nursery class teacher in a Midlands primary. Latterly deputy at a 40 place nursery
Deputy head	Gloria Cert Ed.	Appointed by previous head as a sound practitioner. Wary of new developments in pre-school education.
Teacher	Diane BA, PGCE	5 years' experience, all at Goldstone. Sees Gloria as her role model.

CASE STUDY

The nursery environment

This was once a quiet, well-established area but now an increasingly transient population live in the flats and converted houses surrounding the nursery. There are signs of urban decay, few amenities and limited transport links that make access difficult for parents.

Gwen

Young and ambitious, Gwen appeared the ideal choice as the new head of Goldstone Nursery. Six months later people were not so sure. Initially, Gwen had been very friendly with parents and staff alike, and people described her

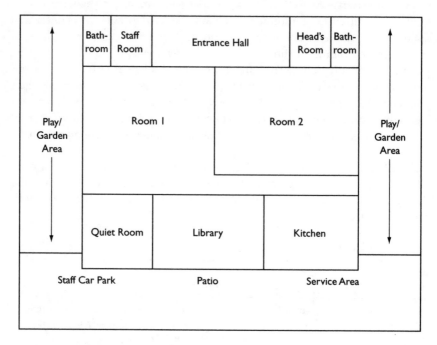

Figure 1.1 Goldstone Nursery

as 'really human' and 'the sort of person you could take your troubles to'. Many of the staff began to say that they were glad that she had been appointed, although in the beginning they would have preferred Gloria to be the new head. Things began to change when Gwen began to be perceived as 'moody' and her behaviour changed from being friendly to 'bossy' with the staff. Furthermore, membership of various Local Education Authority (LEA) steering committees in her first headship caused concern regarding her long-term commitment.

Gloria

Gloria, the teacher in Red Room, had been at Goldstone longer than anyone, and was well liked. After much soul-searching Gloria applied for the headship, and was naturally upset by her own failure to get the post. She often pointed out Gwen's faults to the other staff, saying it was clear that Gwen was not experienced enough to manage such a difficult nursery.

Gloria's resentment had begun when Gwen had reprimanded her for not implementing a change to 'milk times', which, according to Gwen, would be more effective than the current procedure, where staff and children sat together for about 15 minutes quietly talking, drinking and eating snacks. Another issue that Gloria drew to the staff's attention was the time Gwen spent elsewhere talking to other people instead of working alongside her own staff.

Misunderstandings and differences

The problems created by Gwen's unplanned absences were many, and the staff began to notice incidents occurring that could directly affect children's safety. An event that increased anxieties during one of Gwen's absences was when a member of the public called to say that a child was crying in the patio area, where nobody was on duty. According to Gloria this was the direct result of Gwen's absence. As Gwen's deputy Gloria knew she was responsible for what had happened, but she felt let down by Gwen and felt that the situation was Gwen's fault. Gloria decided not to tell anyone about the incident and planned to supervise the nursery more carefully in future, regardless of whether Gwen was there or not. As a result she stopped access to some areas at certain times, particularly over the lunchtime period when staff were in short supply. Registration was another area of disagreement where Gloria felt justified in keeping children seated for a considerable length of time while staff checked the register.

Following this incident, Gwen was furious to find all outdoor provision deserted when she brought round a party of visitors on what was the hottest day of the year. Fifty children and four staff were cooped up in the two large rooms with barriers across the doors to prevent children going into the garden.

Gwen's response

Gwen held a staff meeting soon after this to share her feelings with staff. Diane, who was usually very mild, blurted out that the staff no longer knew what they were up to and they had decided that, in the interests of the children's safety, they should plan around Gwen's constant absences. After the meeting Gwen began to reflect on the past six months since taking up her appointment. She felt that things had been going quite well although she knew she had been over-friendly at first with the staff and, after several incidents in which people seemed to be taking her for granted, she had become more distant with both staff and parents. Reluctantly, she had to concede that things were not progressing so well and that some of Diane's criticisms might be justified. Finally, she admitted to herself that she didn't always feel fully in control and reflected that it was no wonder that staff made up their own rules.

REFLECTION (1)

Think about Gwen's behaviour and try to identify:

What went wrong?
Why it went wrong?

Management style

From the case study you can see that the staff reaction was a direct consequence of Gwen's performance as a manager. In order to identify how to resolve issues such as these it is important to begin by reviewing Gwen's style of leadership. In order to do this it may be helpful to consider the following definitions of leadership and management:

> **Leadership** is the process of influencing the activities of an organised group towards goal setting and goal achievement.
>
> adapted from Stogdill, R. (1974) *Leadership, membership and organization*

> **Leadership** – The behaviour of an individual when s/he is directing the activities of a group towards a shared goal.
>
> adapted from Fiedler, F. (1967) *A theory of leadership effectiveness*

> **Management** – Working with people to plan, organise and control activities in order to accomplish agreed goals.
>
> adapted from Fayol, H. (1986) *General and industrial management*

Clearly all definitions include a degree of overlap, a point discussed by Yukl (1989) who quotes other sources in suggesting that 'managers are concerned about how things get done, and leaders are concerned with what the things mean to people'. Thus, leaders appear to have a stronger influential role among people, one which increases commitment, whereas managers carry out their responsibilities according to their position and exercise authority. Shea (1993) has attempted to highlight these subtle differences, as Table 1.2 shows.

Looking back at the case study, we can apply these rules to Gwen's behaviour (Table 1.3).

Similarly, if Gwen had examined her role as a manager – as shown in Table 1.4 – she might have found gaps.

Table 1.2 The roles of leaders and managers

Leader	Manager
inspires	controls
thinks	does
motivates	organises
initiates change	accepts current practice
dictates	administers
takes decisions	follows through
sets objectives	coordinates
sets the pace	motivated by discipline
inspires loyalty	
self sufficient	

Source: Shea 1993.

Table 1.3 Gwen as a leader

Leader	Gwen's current behaviour	Ideal behaviour would be to
inspires	inspiration is kept for people outside	talk about her 'vision' with her own staff
thinks	thinks about new ways of doing things	share her ideas with staff, encourage their ideas
motivates	confuses staff by her absences	motivate staff by involving them with visitor(s)
initiates change	introduces changes which staff resist	involve staff in the planning so they want the change
dictates	deaf to staff's concerns and tells them what to do	listen to staff and negotiate with them
takes decisions	disruptive and changes things; causes people to think she is dismissive of the past	consult staff to find out why practices have developed in the way they have
sets objectives	fails to be clear about what will happen next	hold meetings with staff to plan long/short term
sets the pace	out on her own, separated from staff	lead team towards attainable goals
inspires loyalty	confuses staff, first too 'matey' then 'stand-offish'	give clear messages to staff at meetings and with individuals
self sufficient	indicates that she doesn't need the help and support of staff	show her staff that she respects their opinions and can handle constructive criticism

Table 1.4 Gwen as a manager

Manager	Gwen's current behaviour	Ideal behaviour would be to
controls	makes her staff uncertain about what she expects	have procedures in place that are understood by everybody
does/organises	unpredictable and does not produce detailed staffing plans	participate more in working with staff in a more practical way
accepts current practices	dismissive of previous patterns of work	examine old practices with staff before establishing a new system of work
administers	unsystematic and as a result does not maintain routine procedures	work with staff on developing a handbook outlining procedures to follow
follows through	unreliable, has lots of ideas but doesn't finish jobs	approach things slowly and systematically
coordinator	good at developing links outside the nursery	give staff opportunities to be involved in making visits and meeting visitors
motivated by discipline	often unpredictable and over-familiar with some staff	establish agreed rules for staff behaviour

---

REFLECTION (2)

How often does your current behaviour fall short of the 'ideal'?

Whether as leader or manager the following general guidelines may be useful in identifying ways to change current behaviour to match your ideal behaviour:

- Remain flexible to ideas within the school or nursery and amend them (rather than abort them without a very good reason).
- Scan the environment and encourage staff to consider new ways based on the practices seen in other schools and nurseries.
- Refine the ideas from outside, be creative in transferring and amending programmes to fit into your targets.
- Provide regular feedback for staff based on visitors' comments as a means of support and further action.
- Create opportunities for team work and leadership in those areas where staff feel confident.
- Develop staff autonomy through a culture of openness, loyalty and improvement.

- Record individual responsibilities and publish realistic goals for all to share.

Audit yourself

Use the information in Tables 1.3 and 1.4 to help you identify your own behaviour by completing Figure 1.2.

So far we have looked at specific skills. Below are some broad descriptions of desirable managerial qualities taken from Hickman and Silva (1988), whose text *Creating Excellence* provides a fresh approach to the role of the leader. As they say, the one essential characteristic of the New Age is change, of which everyone in education has had direct experience over the last decade. Just as important, the authors devote two chapters to building and assessing culture and matching strategy and culture. In their view, long-term success and excellence are brought about through an 'alloy of superior strategies and strong cultures' (p. 78). Read the following descriptions of **creative insight**, **sensitivity**, **versatility and focus** and **vision** and decide how useful they are to you in considering your own performance as a manager.

Creative insight – what does it mean?

Creative insight involves asking penetrating questions; holding open discussions that allow people the freedom to disagree with you; entertaining new ideas that may be different from your own and visualising all possible viewpoints.

In the case study this could involve a discussion about current ways of working

Current behaviour	Ideal behaviour	Points for action

Figure 1.2 Audit form

and the issue of set times for registration and snacks. Listening to and interpreting staff answers would have given an indication of how strongly these practices were tied up in the tradition of the nursery. Often, discussions about such traditions naturally lead to anxiety and a tendency to hang on to old ways. Open discussions can be painful but can indicate that problems are developing. Gwen would have been wise if she had encouraged staff to voice their disagreements so that real communication could begin, whereas what happened was that staff talked about her behind her back, while she dictated to them. Thinking about her attitude to new ideas and realising that in the last few months her behaviour has been unfair should indicate to Gwen that she should have greater awareness of the needs of others.

discussion, however painful, is better than dictating

Sensitivity – what does it mean?

This means recognising the need to discuss other people's expectations rather than assuming you know best. It means treating people as individuals and taking account of their differences; recognising changes and improvements in staff and realising that other people may not respond in the same way as you.

Gwen should realise that where sensitivity is concerned she has a lot to learn. She assumes that she knows best when it comes to making decisions, but she must learn to recognise that she has failed to treat people as individuals. Furthermore, her staff had made many adjustments in order to adapt to her, the new head teacher, as well as accepting other minor changes without protest, while she had done little to be sensitive to them.

Versatility and focus – what do these mean?

These involve developing and trying new methods rather than allowing inflexibility or complacency to settle in; monitoring the environment for changes in ways of working by others. It means deciding which people, structures and skills need to change. It means keeping the right people.

In order to have versatility and focus Gwen would have had to get a lot of other things right first. She should have known that trying new methods would only lead to success if the staff had been able to identify shared goals to achieve, rather than those she had imposed on them, which naturally they had rejected. She should have been sufficiently observant of people's feelings in order to prevent Diane's outburst at the staff meeting. She should also have known that in order to get the best from her staff she should have started by getting to know them better as individuals.

new methods are effective only if the staff identify with them, accept them

Vision – what is it?

Having vision means being able to articulate your own philosophy to a range of people. It means also that you need to be receptive to, and supportive of,

vision → ability to articulate your philosophy to a range of people

new ideas coming from elsewhere. You must pay attention to strengths. It means having a dialogue, talking about future goals and identifying where the opportunities and the dangers may lie.

Gwen had a strong personal philosophy that would have proved invaluable as head of Goldstone Nursery, but her failing was in allowing her own views to stifle any new ideas from other people. She didn't recognise others' strengths and she had been dazzled by the prospects of further opportunities. The result *not antic* was that she had not anticipated the pitfalls that lay ahead. *pitfalls*

You may prefer to use these headings as a method of assessing your own performance as a manager and a leader. Figure 1.3 gives the headings and provides a useful way of reflecting on your previous performance and planning your future strategy.

REFLECTION (3)

Which descriptions of management leadership styles are most useful for you?

	Past examples	Points for action
Creative insight (*Entertaining new ideas, visualising all possible viewpoints from others*)		
Sensitivity (*Recognising the changes and improvements made by staff*)		
Vision (*Being clear about your views of the future and sharing them with staff*)		
Versatility and focus (*Developing new methods to aid your plans*)		
Patience (*Remembering that everything takes longer than you think*)		

Figure 1.3 Categories for management assessment and planning

Managing yourself and managing your time

One of the most important areas of work for any person is time management. People can 'grow' into jobs, but all too often the routines they establish are not necessarily the most effective. A regular review of how you use your time is always valuable. Furthermore, the opportunity to obtain some kind of feedback should never be overlooked.

Outlined below is an alternative approach to time management based on research undertaken with effective managers in industry. We have amended the categories to provide you with a starting-point and some ideas for your own work. In discussions with us regarding the time spent on various aspects of management activity, teachers and other education managers found it helpful to look at the headings in Figure 1.5. We found approximately one-tenth of a week to be the right balance for networking. Traditional management, as defined in Figure 1.4, should normally occupy a little more time, with the substantive elements being allotted to the two key areas of human resource management and routine tasks. Clearly, no week is ever the same and consequently we are reluctant to be more prescriptive. However, we do suggest that you record your activities over a number of weeks, first in list form and then as a pie chart for ease of comparison. Remember, time is a tool that you must use in your own effective way.

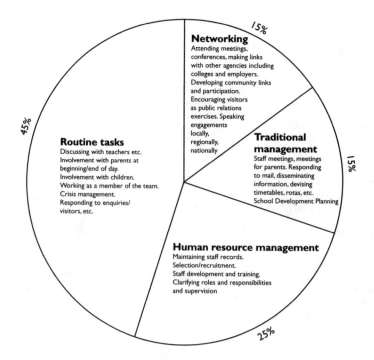

Figure 1.4 The four areas of management

ACTIVITY

Log the amount of time you spend using the headings below (Figure 1.5):

Time management exercise

Networking	Traditional management	Human resource management	Routine tasks

Figure 1.5 Time management exercise

Now compare your time allocation with the pie chart and then complete the chart that follows (Figure 1.6).

Areas to increase	Areas to reduce

Figure 1.6 Points for action

The four areas highlighted in the pie chart (Figure 1.4) indicate the proportion of time that can be given to different tasks and may be used as a rough guide as to how much time senior staff in early years settings could give to various tasks.

Once again we must stress that time management is and always will be a highly individual aspect of management performance. The categories we have included are based on Luthans' (1988) book *Real Managers* and are designed to be a starting-point for reflection.

Having studied the pie chart, now log the amount of time you spend on any activity during a working week. When you have recorded it you need to consider how it breaks down and how effectively it works for you.

REFLECTION (4)

How do you use your time?

Becoming a more effective leader

Throughout this chapter we have stressed guidelines for consideration as ways of improving your performance. Our final section, adapted from Bryman (1986), tries to summarise some of our views and acts as a guide to the following chapters.

1   **Tolerance** – Develop your tolerance of others. Be sensitive to the needs of others and changing situations.

(See chapter 5 – Managing the challenge of change)

2   **People and tasks** – Show high concern with both people and tasks. Combining both things is the most effective managerial strategy, not one at the expense of the other.

(See chapter 4 – Maintaining staff motivation)

3   **Decision-making** – Choose the most appropriate means for making decisions. Decisions must be accurate/effective and should be carefully matched to existing conditions; generally people prefer a participative approach, so err on this side.

(See chapter 7 – Selecting suitable staff)

4   **Leadership** – Always remember that leadership is never just one way. Give and take.

5   **Flexibility** – Above all, be flexible and turn any crisis into an opportunity.

No single approach or strategy is best – methods need to be adapted to suit the situation and the best leaders are the most adaptable ones. Always remember:

*   Know the capabilities of your school or nursery.
*   Motivate your staff.
*   Respond positively to change inside and out.
*   Develop long-term goals and see them through.
*   Turn any crisis into an opportunity.

We have now looked at some of the key areas of leadership and interpreted management theories against a background of issues that might arise within an early years setting. If you would like to extend your knowledge, or follow up a particular theme, the following source books will be helpful.

Further reading

We chose to focus on three books when we wrote this chapter since each offered considerable insights into the ingredients of successful management and leadership.

The first, *Creating Excellence* (1988) Craig Hickman and Michael Silva,

Creating excellence; Craig Hickman + M. Silva

was written to teach people some of the practical skills they need to acquire before they have major leadership responsibilities. The book begins by focusing on excellence within organisations and discusses how leaders create and seek to maintain such excellence. The key words strategy and culture are emphasised because – in the words of the writers – 'although it takes a tremendous investment of time and effort' anyone can learn to achieve them (a heartening message for those faced with considerable challenges in pre-school settings).

contrasting qualities of leaders

The writers go on to identify a number of contrasting characteristics that leaders need to have; they must be visionary yet realistic, sensitive but demanding, innovative yet practical. Next the writers caution about the dangers of 'short termism', that is a preoccupation with immediate results that often cannot be sustained. The type of thinking that only reacts to initiatives is shallow and often ignores essential longer term development planning.

A chapter on strategic thinking follows. A number of examples from the business world on satisfying customer needs, sustaining competitive advantage and capitalising on company strengths are provided, with each example designed to allow a systematic review of what is being undertaken. Once again, there are parallels with an early years service that must continue to be responsive to clients.

The chapter on culture contains a checklist for managers to gauge the level of staff commitment and gives advice on instilling commitment, developing and rewarding competence in key areas and displaying consistency.

The second part of the book develops in detail the theme we touch on in this chapter, so it is appropriate to include a few short quotes to demonstrate the depth of advice offered. 'Creative insight' includes a section on recognising insight, self-examination and removing the blinkers. The quotation 'effective management takes more than intelligence – it takes careful attention to an organization's most valuable asset, its people' sums up the section.

from Hickman Silva

'Sensitivity' reminds us that a position of leadership is not a passport to personal privilege or power: 'The duty of the leader is to serve the needs of those who are led' (p. 135). 'Vision' is defined as a mental journey that 'creates facts, hopes, dreams, dangers'. Clear vision results from a profound understanding of the organisation and its environment. Versatility, anticipating change, and focus, implementing change, reflect the very different approaches that industrial and commercial organisations have towards change in contrast to schools and centres. Nevertheless the chapters contain useful advice and valuable examples of the processes. 'Patience' living in the long term, advocates a necessary long-term approach that will help coordinate all the other managerial skills needed to be effective in the New Age. Clearly there is much business jargon that would benefit from translation into education settings. However, many of the ideas involved are worthy of consideration and adaptation.

The second text we have chosen, **Real Managers** (1988) **Fred Luthans,**

Richard M. Hodgetts and Stuart Rosenkrantz, investigates what 'mainstream managers from middle of the road organizations really do in their day to day activities' and attempts to explain 'how the successful and effective differ from their less successful, less effective counterparts'.

Researched in the United States with a sample of over 450 managers, the authors claim that they make no assumptions about what managers should be doing or could achieve if they were in 'excellent' companies. However, one of the most striking aspects of the book is the attempt to distinguish between the key terms successful and effective. While previously these two terms have been largely synonymous, chapters 3 to 6 explode that myth. Chapter 3 contains a managerial success index based on an employee's seniority level in the company against the time taken to progress.

A checklist for effective managers led to a 16-point list based on the most common references, many of which have limited relevance to education. However, what is important are the priorities given to networking, human resource management and communication by the two categories of manager. To what extent Luthans' research mirrors early years education managers is questionable. Nevertheless, communication, motivation, particularly feedback, and a 'skills for the future' section are examined thoroughly.

A final thought (p. 162) suggests that while few of the managers studied were both successful and effective, those who tried to fulfil such a challenge could not afford to ignore any of the traditional functions of administration (traditional management), communication, networking and human resource management, but also required appropriate feedback to maintain their excellence in the years ahead.

The final recommended book, *Leadership in Organizations* (1989) **Gary Yukl**, is a key text for all those interested in leadership theory. He begins with a definition of leadership, and then discusses its nature, both formal – that is, hierarchical structures such as rank – and informal (see Figure 2.7). Subsequent chapters consider sources of power and control in relation to resources and rewards.

Power, influence, authority and coercion are all discussed as part of tactical leadership. Effective leadership behaviour is considered as well as the path–goal theory of leadership – the effect of a leader in smoothing the way for employees and increasing their 'personal payoffs for work goals attained'. Situational theories that take account of the maturity of the group to be led, as devised by Hersey and Blanchard, are analysed in detail as a basis for attempting a blueprint for effective leadership. 'An integrative model of management behaviour' contains some useful diagrams and quotations to focus the reader on ways that management intervention can improve effectiveness. The section examining managerial motivation and traits as a predictor of effectiveness identifies six areas that are associated with higher motivation (p. 183).

Managers should

1   have a positive attitude towards authority figures;
2   be competitive themselves and for others who work with them;
3   desire to be actively assertive;
4   desire to exercise power;
5   desire to stand out from the group;
6   be willing to carry out routine administrative work.

Charismatic and transformational leadership is discussed, and there are sections on culture and vision in relation to other key writers along with a caution about the darker side of charismatic leadership – behaviour that 'seeks to dominate and subjugate followers by keeping them weak and dependent on the leader'.

In a final overview, Stogdill summarises the wealth and complexity as well as the confusion regarding research on leadership.

> Four decades of research on leadership have produced a bewildering mass of findings . . . The endless accumulation of empirical data has not produced an integrated understanding of leadership.
>
> (Stogdill 1974: 267)

Nevertheless this should not prevent leaders and those aspiring to leadership positions from focusing on strategies for self improvement.

Chapter 2

Working with others

This chapter focuses on: Attitudes and behaviours

                                   Working in groups

                                   Enhancing performance

with examples of how you can identify potential problems with teams and develop individuals so that the team benefits from their strengths.

We examine some of the problems that occur in a school where the staff are understandably nervous when changes are put in place without the benefit of consultation or discussion. We go on to consider ways of developing cohesiveness and ask the reader to think of a familiar scenario – that of the integration of staff for organisational rather than personal reasons. The reader is asked to consider the ways in which individual behaviour and attitudes can be understood; the ways in which groups work and the ways the performance of groups impact on organisational effectiveness.

Groups are defined as two or more people who work together to achieve a common purpose. For many of us they provide the status, security and social relations that make work satisfying, rewarding and, in many cases, pleasurable. We are all tempted, at times, to change jobs, and increasingly in today's climate we may well be forced into changing both our patterns and types of work. As always, few jobs allow us the luxury (if it is one) of working completely on our own. In practice, most of us prefer the balance of being an individual but also of having the security of being a member of a group. When group membership is threatened, or we find ourselves in groups where we do not feel secure, we often react by 'digging in our heels' and refusing to cooperate with others. The type of energy that goes into maintaining this attitude can be destructive and lead to discontent and disaffection, whereas when individuals work together to achieve shared aims, the results of such efforts often far exceed what could have been achieved through the efforts of any one individual.

Following a detailed analysis of the case study the reader is invited to review how effective group work could enhance their performance, both organisationally and individually. The focus then shifts to looking at ways of developing strong group cohesiveness and the reader is encouraged to identify the behaviours that affect, positively or negatively, the way groups interact and perform.

Begin by studying the details of staff (Table 2.1), taking particular note of ages, qualifications and experience and observe the layout of the school building in Figure 2.1.

Table 2.1 Staffing

Staffing role	Name	Age	Qualifications	Experience/Training
Reception Teacher 1	Sally	23	BA (QTS)	Three years Early years trained
Reception Teacher 2	Kath	26	B.Ed.	Four years Early years trained
Nursery Teacher	Andrea	34	B.Ed.	Thirteen years Junior trained
Nursery Nurse 1	Freda	57	NNEB ADCE	Twenty-two years
Nursery Nurse 2	Anna	20	BTec	Two years
Nursery Nurse 3	Maureen	42	NNEB	Seventeen years
Ancillary	Eleanor	38	None	Volunteer

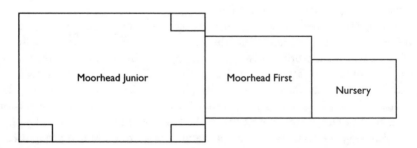

Figure 2.1 Moorhead First and Junior School

CASE STUDY

The school

Moorhead First and Junior School is a large, semi-rural school, which is suf-
fering the results of expansion in the 1970s when many new houses were built
locally. The problems of negative equity and the lack of popularity of the area
to new house-buyers has meant that the school rolls are falling, and in consequence some classes have been amalgamated. This has led to the loss of one
teacher; the re-deployment of another teacher from Key Stage 2 to the early
years team and the temporary employment of a volunteer helper as a paid
ancillary assistant. Following criticisms directed at leadership of the early years
in the school's recent Ofsted inspection, it has also been decided that the
nursery and reception classes should be integrated into a cohesive unit with
shared planning and resources. The head teacher has made some hard
decisions in moving Andrea, a Key Stage 2 teacher, into the early years department and in effectively abolishing the nursery, which was very popular with
the parents. However, she believes that the expertise of her staff is excellent
and she knows that her next task is to get them working together as a
productive group. In view of this she has asked Andrea to lead them in a
series of joint planning meetings. She has, though, seriously underestimated
the attitudes of some of the staff to the changes she has put in place, the
way people work most effectively and the amount of staff development that
will be required before this newly formed group are able to work together
effectively.

The group

The group comprises three teachers, three nursery nurses and one unqualified staff member. The problems faced by them vary, but centre around two
main issues – different perceptions of roles because of differences in pay and
experience between individuals, and resistance, by some individuals, to the
group to which they have been allocated.

Different perceptions of roles

Differences in pay and experience – nursery nurses

The support given to the teachers is both enhanced and restricted by individual differences in the levels of training and the attitudes of the staff members to the types of work they are expected to do. On paper, the three nursery

nurses in the unit differ in almost every way possible. However, closer examination shows that although the nursery nurse who is attached to Reception
I is nearing retirement age, she has been on a variety of courses to update her
earlier training and is very keen to take on new initiatives and offer her skills
to the others. In this way she does not differ greatly from the newly qualified
nursery nurse who wants to develop her skills, and sees the range of her work
as a great opportunity that will allow her to learn. In time, she hopes this will
lead to greater responsibility, under direction from the teacher, in any area of
the curriculum. The third member has a very different approach to the roles
she and her colleagues are given. On the one hand, she argues that she is 'only
a nursery nurse' when she is asked to take part in planning meetings after
school, while, on the other hand, she expects respect for her lengthy experience of working with children.

Ancillary helper

The ancillary helper, the newest staff member, says she just enjoys working
with the children and does not mind doing anything to help anybody.

Differences in experience – teachers

The two reception teachers, Kath and Sally, are both qualified early years
teachers, while Andrea, who has been re-deployed from the upper school, is
trained to work with older children. Kath and Sally strongly believe that it is
inappropriate for Andrea to work in the early years department because she
has not got the specialist knowledge of young children that they possess.

Andrea believes that there are 'good' teachers and she is one of them, her
lessons having been given high ratings in the recent Ofsted inspection. She
believes that the same principles apply to teaching whether the children are
'5 or 15'.

Resistance by individuals to group working

As can be seen from the differences between the individuals in their views of
both themselves and others, there is likely to be considerable resistance to
the work of the group.

Teachers

Clearly, Andrea would have preferred to have remained in the upper school,
where she taught Year 5. Kath and Sally feel her presence is destructive and
an additional burden to them.

They are incensed that the head teacher has asked her to lead the early years staff. Sally is upset because she thinks the head teacher's decision implies a lack of trust, while Kath is more angry because she believes that the head teacher does not value the important work that goes on in the early years. They are both determined to make Andrea's task as difficult as possible.

Andrea, though not happy to move, is pleased with the head teacher's decision to use her leadership skills. Unfortunately, she is not aware that she has a great deal to learn from her colleagues and sees the move as an opportunity to influence things so that children's activities will be more structured and staff will have fewer opportunities for being so 'casual', as she describes their approach to teaching and learning.

Nursery nurses and ancillary helper

There is little real resistance from this group, although all of them fear Andrea's very formal approach to teaching and are concerned that there will be radical changes.

REFLECTION (1)

How can Andrea begin to unite members and build morale?

Figure 2.2 shows task behaviours and suggestions.

All of the suggestions in Figure 2.2 will help the staff understand the benefits of group working. Not only do groups help our sense of belonging, they help us to gain satisfaction in work. Watching and participating both formally and informally helps us to examine, modify and change our ways of working. Hence there are considerable benefits for staff. Figure 2.4 shows how groups impact on individual effectiveness.

Andrea should also be aware of the value of group cohesiveness – the strength and positive attitudes that exist among group members when they pull together. She should also remember the importance of:

Time spent together

- As people spend more time together they can become more tolerant of each other; however, the potential for conflict still remains.

Andrea should try to involve all staff in some of the following:

	Task behaviour	Possible solution
1	**Initiating-contributing** Proposed tasks, goals or actions; defining a problem in a new way; suggesting a procedure or alternative organisation.	Andrea must be careful to demonstrate her competence, coupled with the will to improve.
2	**Information and/or opinion seeking** Asking for relevant facts; asking for clarification of the values underlying the task or suggestions being made.	The skill lies in asking others to reflect on their practice and philosophy. So Andrea should begin to talk to staff about their work.
3	**Information and/or opinion giving** Offering facts; expressing feelings; giving opinions.	Andrea has the security of knowing she is a sound teacher at KS2. This can be translated to help Kath and Sally.
4	**Paraphrasing** Checking on meaning. 'Is this what you mean?' 'If I hear you correctly, you are saying . . .' or 'Let me see if I understand . . .'	It is important that a working vocabulary is established at the outset. Andrea must be prepared to translate some of the shorthand and jargon which she hears in the early years department, some of which will be for effect and some genuinely abbreviated. The more tuned in she becomes to their way of talking, the more she gains group acceptance.
5	**Clarifying and/or elaborating** Interpreting ideas or suggestions; defining terms; clarifying issues before the group; providing examples.	
6	**Summarising and coordinating** Pulling together related ideas; re-stating suggestions; offering a decision or conclusion for the group to consider.	
7	**Reality testing and/or standard testing** Making a critical analysis of an idea; testing an idea against some data trying to see if the idea would work; suggesting standards for the group to achieve in terms of the task.	Identifying ways of planning used successfully in the past that might be usefully adapted.
8	**Recording** Providing the 'group memory' by writing down key points, suggestions and/or decisions.	Andrea should record the thoughts of the group so that they have something to refer back to after meetings.

Figure 2.2 Suggestions for improving morale

ACTIVITY

Use these headings to review your performance when you next lead a meeting.

Task behaviour	
1 **Initiating-contributing** Proposed tasks, goals or actions; defining a problem in a new way; suggesting a procedure or alternative organisation.	
2 **Information and/or opinion seeking** Asking for relevant facts; asking for clarification of the values underlying the task or suggestions being made.	
3 **Information and/or opinion giving** Offering facts; expressing feelings; giving opinions.	
4 **Paraphrasing** Checking on meaning. 'Is this what you mean?' 'If I hear you correctly, you are saying . . .' or 'Let me see if I understand . . .'	
5 **Clarifying and/or elaborating** Interpreting ideas or suggestions; defining terms; clarifying issues before the group; providing examples.	
6 **Summarising and coordinating** Pulling together related ideas; re-stating suggestions; offering a decision or conclusion for the group to consider.	
7 **Reality testing and/or standard testing** Making a critical analysis of an idea; testing an idea against some data trying to see if the idea would work; suggesting standards for the group to achieve in terms of the task.	
8 **Recording** Providing the 'group memory' by writing down key points, suggestions and/or decisions.	

Figure 2.3 Meeting performance review

I	Talking informally helps you to learn about the nursery or other workplaces as well as changes in the environment.	Together staff can begin to understand and appreciate some of the difficulties that arise through job changes and working conditions.
2	Helps you to learn about yourself.	Working more closely together encourages greater feedback and more understanding of one another.
3	Provides help in gaining new skills.	This can be achieved by supporting one another in new circumstances and learning from each other.
4	Gives access to rewards of working with others.	Increased self-esteem gained through the success of the group can lead to feelings of status and satisfaction which in turn lead to higher motivation and personal development.
5	Satisfies important personal needs, especially needs for social acceptance and affiliation.	

Figure 2.4 The impact of groups on individual staff effectiveness
Source: Adapted from Luthans 1985

- They talk and respond and engage in other interactions.
- These interactions lead to a discovery of common interests and increased attraction.

Similarly, she should be aware of the danger presented by:

External threats

Group cohesiveness will increase if the group comes under attack from external sources. Andrea needs to be aware that this goes some way to explaining staff resistance.

Maintaining cohesiveness

She should also seek to maintain cohesiveness through a range of actions shown in Figure 2.5.

Discouraging ineffective behaviour

Finally, and just as important, Andrea should take steps to discourage ineffective behaviour, as highlighted in Figure 2.6.

I	**Encouraging** Being friendly, warm and responsive to others; indicating by facial expression or remark the acceptance of others' contributions.
2	**Harmonising** Attempting to reconcile disagreements; reducing tension; getting people to explore differences.
3	**Gate keeping** Helping to keep communication channels open; facilitating the participation of others; suggesting limits on length of presentations to give everyone a chance to communicate.
4	**Consensus testing** Asking to see if the group is nearing a decision; 'kite flying' to test a possible conclusion.
5	**Compromising** When a personal idea or status is involved in a conflict offering a compromise that yields status; admitting error; modifying in interest of group cohesion or growth.
6	**Standard setting** Suggesting standards for the group to achieve in terms of how well the group works together.
7	**Process observing** Making observations of group processes and supplying this information for group evaluation of its own functioning.
8	**Following** Going along with the movement of the group; serving as an audience in group discussions.

Figure 2.5 Maintenance behaviour
Source: Luthans 1985

ACTIVITY

Having studied these examples try to identify aspects of group behaviour in your work setting. Analyse what effects this behaviour has on the group. Use Figures 2.5 and 2.6 to help you.

Group tasks versus individual work

The challenge for any group leader is to ensure that the tasks lend themselves to effective group working. Robert Baron (1986) refers to 'distraction-conflict

1	**Attacking (aggressive behaviour)** Deflating others' status; attacking the group or its values; joking in a barbed or semi-concealed way; trying to take credit for another's contribution.
2	**Blocking** Disagreeing and opposing beyond 'reason'; resisting stubbornly the group's wish for personally orientated reasons; using hidden agenda to thwart the movement of a group.
3	**Dominating** Asserting authority or superiority to manipulate the group or certain of its members; interrupting contributions of others; controlling by means of flattery or other forms of patronising behaviour.
4	**Playboy/playgirl behaviour** Making a display in 'playboy/playgirl' fashion of one's lack of involvement; 'abandoning' the group while remaining physically with it, perhaps through cynicism or nonchalance.
5	**Recognition-seeking** Calling attention to oneself through boasting or reporting on one's achievements.
6	**Self-confessing** Using the group to express non-related personal feelings, insights, ideologies.
7	**Sympathy-seeking** Attempting to arouse sympathy through expressions of insecurity or self-deprecation.
8	**Special-interest pleading** Speaking for the 'small businessman', the 'housewife', 'labour', etc.; frequently hiding one's own biases behind a convenient stereotype.

Figure 2.6 Ineffective behaviour
Source: Adapted from Benne and Sheats 1948

theory'; how the presence of an audience can create a conflict of attention among people performing a task. His example refers to proof-readers becoming distracted by each other, and could just as easily apply to staff in a busy nursery.

Working in the presence of others is an important consideration for all managers and something that leads to varying results. Research has shown that under some conditions it can lead to improved performance. This is often when teachers/nursery nurses or assistants are familiar with what they are doing and, knowing that they are being watched, do it better or quicker. However there is a danger that in a group situation some people will switch off, thinking they won't be noticed. Such 'loafing around' is often a sign of boredom or stems from a belief that an individual's efforts will go unnoticed. Just as in a large group of children some will 'coast' around the activities, so the same can apply

ACTIVITY

Review the tasks currently being undertaken by groups in your establishment. Can you identify examples of:

- distraction
- apprehension about evaluation
- evidence of 'social loafing around'?

REFLECTION (2)

In what ways can group working be improved in your setting?

to helpers in a group situation. The challenge for the manager is to be aware of the situation and devise a range of tasks, some of which require feedback.

Further reading

We have again chosen a book by Luthans in addition to two further texts for discussion. *Organizational Behaviour* (1985) **Fred Luthans** is a compendium that has provided us with considerable background information and ideas. The chapter on groups reproduces Homan's theory on group formation which identifies interaction activities and sentiments as an integral part of group effectiveness, with the former being the most important. As Luthans says, 'Persons in a group interact with one another . . . to solve problems, attain goals, facilitate co-ordination, reduce tension and achieve a balance'.

It is from this text that we have adapted Figure 2.7, 'Informal roles of staff in early years settings'. Although the categories are broad and somewhat superficial statements, they nevertheless provide a further starting-point for recognition and understanding of group behaviour.

The balance theory, that persons are attracted to one another on the basis of similar attitudes, is an important consideration for the manager and worthy of note in decisions about recruitment and selection. Luthans returns to research from the Hawthorne studies (an experiment involving young girls working on an assembly line in the 1920s who were subject to changed patterns of working as a basis for increasing productivity) to stress the importance of affiliation. As he says, 'Most often formal organizational arrangements do not satisfy the important social needs'. Group cohesiveness is examined in terms of the role of the leader with the conclusion that 'A highly cohesive group that is given positive leadership will have the highest possible productivity'. On the other hand, a highly cohesive group that is given poor leadership will have the lowest

Those that say:

It needs doing, so let's get on with it – for example developing planning models, changing the system of record keeping or re-assessing the approach to reading, are task-orientated.

This is how to do it – for example managing stock or resources so that there is a systematic and fair approach to using and ordering materials, are systems people.

I am a people-person – and choose to work with parents or to be 'keyworker' to vulnerable children.

Whatever it is I'm against it – 'nay sayers' are usually people who are fearful of change and choose to hold on to familiar practices because they feel most confident with the things they have done previously.

We'll find a way to do it – this group, 'yes sayers', usually find a way round a problem and will do their best to overcome opposition.

Rules are to be kept and are never negotiable – we go by the book here. A useful position for inflexible workers who see things from a very narrow perspective (rule enforcers).

We know the rules are there, but we don't always follow them to the letter – this group may 'bend' rules or even ignore them, and depending upon their motivation may be helpful or otherwise (rule blinkers).

You can count on me – this group of regulars forms the backbone of any establishment, the silent majority who get on with the job.

Life begins when this place closes – these semi-detached people are often the ones who follow the rules, working sufficiently during the set hours, but unwilling to do any more.

I'm not the same as everyone else – these people are often loners and sometimes see themselves as the subject of unfair treatment, or as being superior to the rest of the group.

I'm learning the ropes – path-finders are often newly qualified, or students who fit in with the establishment.

I've seen it all before – people who have worked in the field for a long time and believe that there is nothing new, and little left to learn (old timers).

Figure 2.7 Informal roles of staff in early years settings
Source: Adapted from Luthans 1985

productivity. Clearly there are considerable limitations in the validity of such results as they affect early years settings but there is nevertheless much to assimilate in this section.

Three other areas are also worthy of notice. First, the section on 'group think', the characteristic that suggests a group may often make more risky decisions than individuals – a point related to Baron's work in a variety of groups. Second, the section on the informal roles of employees within organisations; while certain terms like 'nay sayers' might appear somewhat alien, their behaviour is often familiar to education, so much so that we include an amended set of categories. Finally, the section on the role of groups in informal communication and group behaviour in committees overlaps with chapter 6, hence it is sufficient to record that a grapevine can not only provide satisfaction and stability to groups but can also sometimes lighten a manager's formal workload by sealing some of the gaps in the communication chain.

Our next choice is **Behaviour in Organizations** (1986) **Robert Baron**. This book was revised to contain a new chapter on group dynamics which provided the focus for many of our ideas. Each of the four sections contains a number of fundamental issues beginning with characteristics and norms, followed by a discussion of roles and their competing demands. Baron's section on working in the presence of others is an area that we address only briefly yet in no way diminish. Equally, his interpretation of Zajonc's (1980) research regarding the presence of others as an influence in completing tasks has considerable importance in an early years setting. Zajonc concluded that 'one may be expected to perform better on a task in the presence of others if that task is very well learned'. However, for unfamiliar activities the presence of others is seen as a hindrance, something to take account of when introducing new procedures. Baron's explanation considered not just the presence of others but a person's fear of being evaluated as another key aspect. Just as important was the distraction element caused by people being around, often no more than the inevitable small-talk that occurs.

The other important area for discussion is the varieties of group tasks. Here again there are important messages for the education manager in identifying which processes lend themselves to group working and which are better kept to individuals.

The typology (amended here for education) is as follows:

Additive   Several people contributing to a workshop or to planning the curriculum.

Compensatory   Accepting the variable contributions of several members of staff to the handbook for parents or to a display.

Disjunctive   Selecting one nursery officer's approach to parents as a model to be used throughout the nursery.

Conjunctive   Working slowly to develop practice in equal opportunities, for example, in order to take everybody along together, rather than rushing at writing a policy that some people will have difficulty in 'owning'.

First, such categories and their analysis provide interesting insights on individual temptations towards social loafing (not pulling one's weight) and offer managers suggestions for counteraction. As Baron says, 'we are not likely to loaf if we believe we may get caught loafing'. Second, they show the benefit of compromise in compensatory group tasks as an ingredient towards greater accuracy. Third, the necessary explanations needed to establish that one person has achieved the right answer can provide an important check on procedures. Finally, the dangers of being slowed down by individuals in groups, whether in report writing, completion of records or projects should encourage managers to think carefully when establishing and encouraging blanket group procedures. Baron's chapter ends with a glossary of key terms that stands alone as an important aid. The fact that he chose to include additional material in his last revision is a testament to the importance he places on this area of human behaviour for, as he says, 'work groups have been found to have a major impact on the functioning of organizations' not least in an early years setting.

Our last text in this section, **Working in Organizations** (1988) **Andrew Kakabadse, Ron Ludlow and Susan Vinnicombe**, provides a valuable guide for any manager faced with the issues of organising, leading and developing effective relationships. The impact of power and the effect of various structures on values and attitudes are considered over twelve chapters with the text divided into two parts: 'People, Jobs and Relationships' and 'Working in the Organization'.

Chapter 6 of the book – Groups – discusses formal and informal groups and their ten main uses, along with comments on size and structure. Group dynamics and individual needs are highlighted by a process model that demonstrates the transformational nature of the group process. The ongoing case studies act as a focus to discuss various characteristics of group behaviour which, despite being set in a construction firm, nevertheless share similarities with early years settings.

Later parts of the chapter concentrate on the stages of group development and behaviour, with four outline strategies designed to improve group performance:

1 Help members to become acquainted. The authors emphasise the leader as facilitator and task initiator, and claim that 'working on particular jobs is less threatening to individuals and also gives each person in the group a feeling of accomplishment'.

2 Help members to offer feedback. An understanding of the inevitable causes of friction and conflict brought on by struggles for power and leadership is essential, as are mechanisms to provide sensitive yet honest feedback. Both are ways of improving relationships.

3 Help members to establish criteria. This needs discussion and guidance as the group matures and so becomes more independent and less sensitive to criticism.

4 Help members to take part in the running of the group and the development of its members. Responsibilities here lie close to the boundaries of teambuilding and might prove difficult to attain.

It is worth consulting the two checklists, self-orientated behaviours and dimensions of group competence. Behaviours like the four help-points provide a framework for diagnosing staff behaviour. Sadly, a column giving guidelines for appropriate responses is not included. Dimensions of group competence can be used both during and after group tasks as a basis for review and evaluation. Again, thought needs to be given towards appropriate remedies but the background knowledge supplied is an invaluable support.

Chapter 3

Teams and team building

This chapter focuses on: The ways in which teams differ from groups
Ways to develop teams
Strategies for successful team building

with examples of how team-building programmes can improve the
effectiveness of schools and centres.

The first step in team building is to help team members become aware of what they do and how others respond to their actions, attitudes and behaviours. Teams go through a number of phases or stages in which members learn to recognise one another's strengths and weaknesses; begin to find ways of working together; begin to communicate their feelings and find a team 'spirit' or ethos, in which the needs and aspirations of the team have priority over those of individuals.

In the case study that follows the reader is invited to note the stages which need to be worked through in forming a new team and how the skills of all staff are developed through the thoughtful intervention of a leader.

Begin by studying the details of staff in Table 3.1.

CASE STUDY

Millwood Educare Centre is a new nursery based in a busy town. It is owned privately and the proprietor has recently appointed a large number of staff including a manager and a deputy manager.

The nursery is on a main road near to a major road which gives access to the motorway. The surrounding buildings are mature and there are trees all

Table 3.1 Staff details

Name/Staffing role	Qualifications	Experience/Training
Elise Nursery Manager	ADCE NNEB	9 years working through from officer to deputy
Jackie Deputy	BTEC NN	7 years in various settings
8 Nursery Officers	all NNEB	variety of experience with babies, toddlers, 3+s
2 domestics/ cooks	Food handling and hygiene	experiences in a variety of commercial and industrial settings

around. Parents are competing for places at the nursery and willing to pay considerable amounts of money for places for their children.

The nursery and its owner

The nursery is owned by an intelligent woman who has excellent business skills and recognises the importance of providing good-quality childcare and education for working parents. She is very fond of children and has had her own family, although she has no formal training in childcare or education. She is keen to expand her 'empire' and plans, if this nursery is successful, to open a second one within twelve months. The purpose-built building is light and airy; space is minimal, although within the guidelines offered by the local authority. The play area is pleasant, if small, and offers children a variety of surfaces, some mature trees, bushes and flowers.

The team

The proprietor has recruited qualified staff so that the nursery is seen as a model of good practice. She has chosen Elise as manager because she believes Elise's philosophy to be very similar to her own and she thinks that her wide experience will enable her to lead the team well. The deputy has not had as much experience as Elise but she is very enthusiastic and has good experience of working with older children; she is particularly keen to develop the curriculum for these children. The remaining staff are all experienced in that they have each had at least two years working in crèches, private nurseries or local authority provision, and they all came across as keen and enthusiastic in their interviews.

Building a team

The nursery team have had little time to work together before their official opening. This has been because of the finance involved in employing such a large staff before beginning to see any return on investment. As a result the proprietor has given Elise one month on full pay to set up the nursery, and has employed two of the nursery officers to come in part-time to help set up during the week before opening. In addition she has paid the deputy for the equivalent of one week's salary so that she and the manager can begin to work on policies and procedures. Because of the way the nursery has been organised the only time the whole staff have been able to meet together has been on the Friday prior to the Monday opening. The focus of this day was procedures, although Elise had tried to spend some time with each group of staff in their separate rooms so that they and she felt confident about working with one another. However, in spite of everything being in place, staff still felt that they had to get themselves organised in their rooms ready for the 'big day' on Monday. The result is that through having to work together in this way the staff have quickly 'bonded' in each of the rooms, without really feeling any sense of the wider team in which they are working.

REFLECTION (1)

How can Elise make the groups in the babies' room, the toddlers' room and the other areas feel part of a wider team?

In the case study it can be seen that unless Elise starts as she means to go on, the team may end up as several groups, all of whom may be strongly committed to their work but none of whom may feel they are part of the wider team. It is important for Elise to have a 'vision' that she wants to achieve. Her task is to look at where the team is now and plan where she wants them to progress to. Before embarking on a team-building cycle it would be helpful to look at some of the characteristics of an undeveloped team as any team leader must recognise some of the symptoms of an undeveloped team before she or he is able to build their team. Table 3.2 shows some of these symptoms and possible solutions.

When a leader takes on a new team it is important to find ways of building success and morale.

Team-building cycle

Ordinarily, a team-building programme will follow a cycle similar to that depicted in Figure 3.1. The whole programme begins because someone recognises a problem or problems. Figures 3.1 and 3.2 show the processes involved in the task of team building and exemplify a possible process for Elise to follow.

Table 3.2 The characteristics of an undeveloped team

Symptoms	Examples	Possible solutions
Task orientated	Each group of staff is focused on getting things right for 'their' children.	Some staff could work flexibly between rooms.
People conform to the established line	A strong 'work ethos' develops which prevents informal relationships developing.	More discussion of the importance of taking time out in order to increase own energy and make contacts with other staff members.
Leadership is seldom challenged	All staff feel new and unsure of both themselves and one another and are coming to terms with a new job.	Elise should consider encouraging staff from each room to represent the views of their group at staff meetings. In this way no individual will feel that they are likely to be identified as unwilling to be led.
No shared understanding	Because all the staff have such different experiences and there has been little time to develop as a team they may only share the fact that they have all trained to work with children.	The policies and procedures which were put in place in order to meet legal requirements will need to be reviewed very quickly. So this is a good opportunity for Elise to get the staff together to write new policies/amendments reflecting their beliefs.
People confine themselves to their own job	This has happened most obviously in the baby room because of the one-to-one care they are required to give to the very youngest children, which restricts them from mixing with other staff.	Elise should begin to consider ways of defining roles and responsibilities so that all staff have an interest in the nursery beyond the room they work in. She could give people roles which mean they are responsible for 'planning' or health and safety throughout the nursery.
The 'boss' takes most of the decisions	Elise has not had sufficient time to know her staff's strengths so she often makes decisions better left to individuals.	Elise should begin by at least consulting staff before making decisions on their behalf.

Action planning

As can be seen from the team-building cycle (Figure 3.1), Elise must begin by thinking about and observing what is happening. She must then analyse what she has discovered so that she can identify the underlying issues. Next, she must consider what action to take. A good action plan will provide her with action points, times in which the action is to be achieved, names of those who

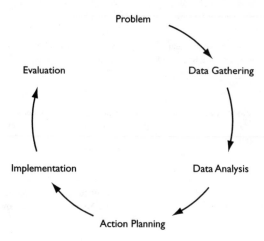

Figure 3.1 The team-building cycle
Source: Adapted from Dyer 1987

are to carry out the tasks and details of how the action is to be implemented and evaluated.

Many of the tasks managers set themselves are part of an action plan, although frequently these are not written down or considered as such. The important point about creating action plans is that the plans should recognise that individuals and groups within the team may have competing priorities; sometimes these priorities conflict so the best way to ensure that everybody feels that their views have been considered is through a discussion of the issues. To begin with, new teams will have very different needs and for most staff their personal needs will be high, which is something that Elise should acknowledge. However, a more established team will almost certainly have different personal and professional interests and priorities.

In his book *Team Building*, William Dyer suggests a simple priority ranking for everyone to complete in which each person, or group, identifies their own priorities. It is very valuable when formulating action plans to have a clear understanding of individual priorities and rankings; Dyer's model (Figure 3.5) can provide a good insight into these.

Elise could ask each of the staff groups to identify their priorities in this way. She may discover that similar priorities exist and she may be able to show staff that their aims are the same. If she finds that their priorities are different she can then help them to recognise which ones are more important than others in the short term.

Often people express a genuine commitment to a particular idea, target or approach, and a chart provides a record of these feelings. Those members of staff who are sceptical about ideas need to be approached individually and given more time to raise concerns. Equally it must be stressed that lukewarm support

Problem Elise wants to lay the foundations for team building which she believes can be improved ⇓	*Action* Find out what is taking place and identify good practice
Data gathering In her visits around the nursery she notes that already there are different ways of working being established ⇓	*Action* Record what is happening and begin to evaluate its effectiveness
Data analysis Elise should analyse what she has discovered to identify the underlying issues ⇓	*Action* To encourage others to observe as a basis for evaluating their own work
Action planning Elise could begin to develop an outline pro forma that lists the activities she would like to see taking place ⇓	*Action* She needs to make staff aware of her commitment by encouraging them to contribute to the lists
Implementation Weekly visits to record a 'file of evidence' to help monitoring ⇓	*Action* Staff consultation on recording methods and format should be encouraged
Evaluation Every 4–6 weeks one member of the group should be asked to evaluate the activities before the support staff rotate	*Action* To ensure that staff evaluate and support staff maintain a flexible approach

Figure 3.2   A team-building process

ACTIVITY

Use the scale in Figure 3.5 to identify priorities within your team and tabulate the results.

(around the middle) is not enough and a certain amount of influencing will be needed. Gillen (1997) summarises the principles of influence very clearly in his skills-based manual (see Figure 3.6).

ACTIVITY

Using Figure 3.3 consider your own situation and how such a cycle can help.

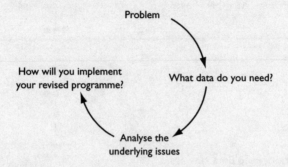

Figure 3.3 An action-plan cycle

Use the headings in Figure 3.4 to formulate an action plan to improve team building in your situation.

1   What are the signs of poor teamwork? (column 1)
2   What will you do? Who will help you? Which tasks seem appropriate? (column 2)
3   What is your preferred style of working? (column 3)
4   What is a realistic timescale? (column 4)
5   What will be your success criteria? (column 5)

1	2	3	4	5
Target action points	*Who will carry out the tasks?*	*How will the action be implemented?*	*When will the action be completed?*	*How will the action be evaluated/by whom?*

Figure 3.4 An action plan

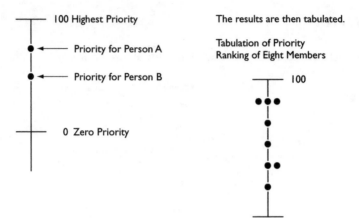

Figure 3.5 Priority and time rankings
Source: Dyer 1987

1	'Pull' don't 'push'	We need the other person to accept the logic of our approach and must try to move the discussion at their pace, not ours.
2	Involve people as much as possible	Encourage them to think through what we are advocating – getting them to think it was their idea!
3	Think behaviour rather than personality	Observe their behaviour rather than labelling their actions. Be consistent in your actions to encourage predictable responses from them.
4	Persuade, don't manipulate	Respect the other person and seek to understand their point of view.

Figure 3.6 The principles of influence
Source: Adapted from Gillen 1997

Working guidelines

Establishing working guidelines is an important stage in the process of building a team ethos because ways of working need to be established at the outset. It is important to consider the following.

How will we make sure everyone has a chance to raise issues and concerns?

Open meetings, agendas and discussion groups can all help but the facilitator needs to ensure that everyone feels their contribution is valued through individual encouragement and feedback. It may be important to encourage everybody to say something and to establish ground rules that state that no contribution is too small and suggest that every contribution is valued. Elise and her deputy need to work hard in order to give all staff such opportunities.

How will differences be resolved?

Conflict is inevitable in any team and can often be healthy. Clear guidelines need to be established concerning acceptable behaviour. This may be achieved through establishing ground rules, for example, only one person may speak at a time, or confidentiality. Time limits are useful but disagreements not dealt with can often lead to increased discontent. This is a vital point for Elise to get right from the beginning so that staff know that the work of teams can be developed through communication rather than through more negative alternatives.

REFLECTION (2)

What are the priorities for your team? How do the priorities of individuals or groups conflict? Can you identify long, medium and short term aims so that everybody's priorities will eventually become team priorities?

Dealing with resistance

Resistance is a predictable outcome of relationships. Whatever the reasons, resistance must be confronted honestly or it will go underground. In this case study most resistance may arise from uncertainty because when people feel insecure they become resistant to change and need to establish a sense of control. This is often when people 'dig in their heels'. Ground rules need to be established to stop destructive behaviour from occurring and recurring. Most important at this stage is to keep open the channels of communication. In a new team it may be difficult for people to be honest and the manager may need to reassure members about confidentiality and her or his commitment to a 'no-blame' approach to different views and beliefs. Figure 3.7 could be used by a team and results recorded by the person chairing the team meeting or, if staff are sufficiently confident, by members sharing their responses. Its purpose is to encourage feedback. The key ingredient is trust, with the leader or facilitator being prepared to face issues that will improve the way the team is developing without creating further problems.

All members complete a sheet and, depending on the level of trust, call out or record their answers to the facilitator. The results can then be analysed in

1   How confident are you that any real change will result from these meetings?

1	2	3	4	5
Not confident at all		Some confidence		High

2   To what degree do you feel the people really want to be here and work on team-development issues?

1	2	3	4	5
Don't really want to be here		Some interest in being here		High interest in being here

3   How willing do you think people are to actually make changes that may be suggested?

1	2	3	4	5
Will be unwilling to change		Some willingness to change		Very willing to change

4   How willing do you think you and others will be to express real feelings and concerns?

1	2	3	4	5
Not very willing		Some degree of willingness		Very willing

Figure 3.7 Feedback sheet

order to discuss group and individual views. Elise, with her own manager, may decide that she should involve her staff in a team-building programme.

Team building – follow up

Dyer states:

> Team building is a process - not an event. Too many team-building programs have failed, not because the initial sessions were ineffective, but due to the lack of clear follow-up to ensure that the gains, agreements, and assignments made had been moved ahead.

> (Dyer 1987)

Simple records of decisions taken, action required and dates for completion can usefully identify ongoing progress in the way follow-up is to be developed. Figure 3.8 can be adapted to record this.

Equally important are regular informal meetings between the team leader and everyone involved. The purpose being to:

Decision	Action by	Completion date

Figure 3.8 Record sheet

- discuss any work problems, and help resolve concerns between team members;
- share any information thought to be relevant;
- help with work issues;
- review events/action points of the last programme and look ahead to future developments.

Team-building programme

An agenda is essential. The following framework, adapted from Dyer (1987), can be used to reduce anxiety and help people focus on the issues.

Team-building agenda

1   **Goals**
    a   What should the goals be for the team-building session?
    b   What should the overall goals be for our unit?
    c   What should the goals be for yourself?
2   **Strategic planning**
    Where do we want to be in 1, 3, 5 years?
3   **Expectations**
    What do we expect of others on the team?
    The management?
    What are the manager's expectations of team members?
4   **Decision making**
    Who makes what decisions?
    How should decisions be made?
5   **Organisation**
    Are we organised appropriately?
6   **Morale**
    What is the current level of morale in our unit?
    How could it be improved?

7 **Relations with other units**
How well are we working with other nurseries/departments, the LEA?

8 **Strengths and weaknesses**
What do we see as our strengths as a unit? Our weaknesses?
How do we correct our weaknesses?

9 **Current problems**
Are there any current problems or concerns not listed that we need to address?

The following examples from the case study illustrate some of the goals Elise and her manager and staff may consider important.

Goals

- An appropriate starting-point in terms of goals for a new nursery would be to develop a mission statement that identifies a commitment to good quality care and education, the importance of partnership with parents and a commitment to equal opportunities.
- Overall goals for the unit may include opportunities for staff to work flexibly, moving between rooms and working with children of all ages for the benefit of children's security, stability and self-esteem.
- Goals for each staff member will be different depending on age, qualifications and ambition. Some staff may have goals associated with improving current performance, while others may wish to undertake a range of new tasks in order to broaden their skills.

Further reading

We have chosen three texts to recommend for further reading, the first of which is *Team Building* (1987) **William Dyer**. This begins with the author puzzling over the fact that while 'almost every manager supports team building and many feel it is essential', very few organisations institute such a programme, furthermore those who do can expect a considerable degree of resistance. Following a review of group characteristics, the section on preparing a team-building programme starts by justifying a diagnosis. Next, there is a checklist for assessment, and finally a number of design options to provide a valuable resource for any manager. The importance of follow-up is summarised in a chapter that reminds us that 'team building means a continuing effort to monitor the team's ability to implement actions designed to improve team performance' and the 'key person is the team leader'. The third part of the book deals with applications of team development and processes for developing the new team.

Practical guidelines on agendas and on operations are followed by a chapter on conflict and negotiation with a view to revitalising a complacent team. Once again, questionnaires and checklists provide practical approaches that lead to a section on reducing inter-team conflict through a facilitator, or working through a clearly structured programme. The final chapters deal with unhealthy agreement brought about by group pressure (sometimes known as the 'Abiline paradox'), and specific people problems in teams. Situations where team building should not be used remind us that a favourable environment, a supportive organisation and a committed manager are all necessary factors if the best efforts are not to be swamped by rejection and apathy.

The book *Positive Influencing Skills* (1997) **Terry Gillen** describes 'non-manipulative persuading behaviours', that enable you to achieve more with other people by enhancing your own credibility rather than relying on authority. The focus for managers, therefore, would be the change to instilling rather than imposing values in people, by agreeing targets, resolving differences of opinion, coaching people and providing feedback, as well as encouraging more two-way communication.

Gillen's fundamental principles centre around the following processes. First, progress with people is better if 'we pull gently at their pace rather than trying to push hard at ours'. Second, involving people is a more effective way of influencing them than talking at them. Third, persuasion, where someone is encouraged to see your point of view, is better than manipulating people and so tricking them into compliance. Fourth, we should avoid labelling people and concentrate on their behaviour rather than their personality. Fifth, as beliefs affect our behaviour we should seek to understand rather than to be understood.

Gillen also outlines five core skills that are independent of the principles and again provide a useful resource toolkit for a manager. First comes probing and listening based on American psychotherapist Carl Rogers' categories to develop questioning and counselling skills. Second, get on the same wave-length through signposting your intentions at the beginning of a sentence and so developing your capacity to synchronise with the other person's thoughts. Third is persuasive selling, identifying with other people's concerns and then responding according to their demands. Fourth, be aware of body language and its impact in all interpersonal and team-building situations; pay particular regard to tone of voice, posture and proximity. Finally, develop assertiveness skills and behaviour to increase personal effectiveness while resisting unacceptable demands. Gillen's final chapters on Gameplans, with guidelines on praising (p. 148) and coaching strategies (p. 178), are all valuable sections that can help team-building programmes become more effective.

Managing Groups and Teams (1996) **Hank Williams** is our third book. It provides managers with a useful sourcebook that covers the most important aspects of interpersonal skills development. Williams begins with the distinction between groups and teams and identifies the degree of collaboration as an important difference; 'It is usually the case that whereas teams need leaders, groups need managers', which, together with issues of involvement, commitment, cooperation and support, distinguish one from another. A chapter on resource needs sees energy, control, expertise and influence as essential ingredients with types of relationship, the nature of the activity, the working environment, previous achievements and the degree of recognition being important supplementary factors. Questions of leadership are considered through the '3D' strategies:

- The Doers who are too busy retaining control over others to develop people.
- The Delegators who because of their concerns for tasks allow others to participate but still invest very little in developing people.
- The Developers who invest considerable time in working with others to motivate and support other people.

Part 2 looks at the strategies needed to manage groups and teams, beginning with meetings, and how one can control without dominating other participants, yet at the same time guarantee an efficient outcome. Individual accomplishment forms another chapter, with sections on recognition and developing authority being the major themes. A final section on interactive skills contains chapters on groupworking skills, dealing with interruptions, invitations and 'telling versus asking', leading to a section on the use and value of questions and proposing ideas. Awareness of avoidance techniques, through a cycle of escalating conflict and negative behaviour, is discussed in terms of providing sensitive feedback and making demands designed to improve behaviour.

As Williams concludes in his summary, all these behaviours are the 'baseline management skills'. They are worth practising as they will help you to manage all your team-building relationships more effectively.

Chapter 4

Maintaining staff motivation

This chapter focuses on: Motivation and how it links to morale
Opportunities for developing individual motivation
through job rotation; job enlargement and job
enrichment

with examples of how this might be achieved in a pre-school setting.

Motivation has been described as 'the will to *want* to do something'. It is the key to success and can be a significant factor in whether an organisation is judged to be effective or ineffective. The way individuals perform in nurseries or schools is often influenced by the degree to which they feel satisfied that their contribution is recognised and valued by management; the extent to which they feel able to develop and progress in their work and their attitudes to their pay and working conditions. In the case study that follows, we will examine the ways in which staff morale can be raised and their contribution valued, so that they do not become de-motivated. It introduces Carol, manager of Under 5s provision in a local authority, whose task is to motivate staff whose job prospects are restricted by changes in local government boundaries.

CASE STUDY

Newholme Local Authority is a new unitary authority in a semi-rural setting close to the West Country. The area is served by one motorway giving access to London, an infrequent train service and a less than reliable bus service. With two nurseries offering full day-care, thirty nursery classes and one nursery school which is awaiting closure, there are some concerns about career

Table 4.1 Roles and career aspirations of the nursery staff

Organisation	Roles/Number of staff	Future career choice
Cedars	Manager 1	To remain in present post
"	Deputy Manager	To become a manager
"	6 FT Nursery Officers	All but two wish to keep present post; two wish to seek promotion in the field
Ashes	Manager 2	To teach Nursery Nurses in FE College
"	Deputy	To have her own nursery
"	4 FT Nursery Officers	One wishes to do a degree in Early Childhood Studies; one to become a Deputy; two wish to keep present post
	2 PT Nursery Officers	Both would like FT work in future

progression. In most cases the staff have worked in the area for their entire careers and although most would not wish to travel, they nevertheless feel that their future progress has been severely curtailed since the large local authority to which they belonged has been dismantled. As a result there is considerable negativity, especially in each of the day nurseries, and many staff complain of being de-motivated. Absence during the Autumn has run much higher than in the previous year. The LEA has appointed Carol as manager to develop early years provision and clearly motivation is high on her list of priorities. Table 4.1 shows the roles and future career choices of staff in the nurseries who work directly with children and families.

Staffing

Carol recognises that *all* her staff are important but is particularly concerned with 'getting things right' in the day nurseries where career opportunities are limited. She is also aware that nursery officers consider their pay and conditions less favourable than those of nursery nurses employed in schools.

The issues

Carol is aware that all staff need to feel that what they do is important, and recognises that not everybody will feel that their needs are a priority for her budget. She knows that unless she can motivate staff the nurseries will not be providing good-quality care for the children. She decides to approach the task of motivating staff by systematically examining their present posts, preferences for their future development and the actions she, as manager, needs to take. The results of an analysis of the staff group are given in Tables 4.2 and 4.3.

In any organisation staff will be at different stages in their career development. Carol discovered that the largest group wished to remain in their posts

Table 4.2 An analysis of the staff at Cedars

Present position	Future choice	Action manager	Staff development
Manager	No change	N/A	Maintain and develop skills
Deputy Manager	Management position	Support by directing her to INSET and providing opportunities to deputise for manager	Management course Deputising for manager
2 Nursery Officers	Promotion	Provide support and advice about training and/or job swaps or shadowing	1 Visiting other nurseries 2 Job shadowing the deputy 3 Acting 'up' in deputy's absence
4 Nursery Officers (wishing to remain in post)	No change	N/A	Maintain and develop skills

Table 4.3 An analysis of the staff at Ashes

Present position	Future choice	Action manager	Staff development
Manager	Teaching (FE)	Support by providing staff cover if opportunities arise for lecturing in FE	1 Continue to supervise Nursery Nurses for their college placements 2 Accept offers to act as visiting lecturer at college 3 Provide INSET to all early years workers to develop teaching skills
Deputy Manager	Manage own nursery	as Cedars' Deputy	Management course Deputising for Manager Financial management
4 FT Nursery Officers	1 Additional training/ study	Support application	Time
	1 Deputy Manager post	Seek opportunities to increase experience	Job swap/acting up
	2 No change	N/A	Maintain and develop skills
2 PT Nursery Officers	Full-time work	Note information	Develop skills

and she therefore concluded that while she must be aware of the future needs of this group, they were not currently high on her list of priorities. The part-time staff seeking full-time work were also in the same category. However, staff seeking promotion or job-related development required specific experiences to support their career progression so Carol saw this group as high on her list of priorities.

Having surveyed her staff, Carol began to develop specific programmes based on their motivation stage in career terms. She believed that each individual had their own personal motivator within them and if this could be unlocked then greater job satisfaction and effective working would result. Carol used Figure 4.1 to help her analyse the career stages of the nursery staff so that she could begin to identify their training needs.

ACTIVITY

Can you use Figure 4.1 to find out the stages that staff are at in either Cedars or Ashes nursery?

Use the same chart (Figure 4.1) to identify the career stages of your own staff then identify possible tasks which would enhance their professional development. Begin by listing staff in order of experience in education/care settings.

Having identified training needs, managers can begin to consider the priorities of the organisation against those of individuals in order to assess how best to allocate spending. However Carol, like many managers, faces the problem that demands for training outstrip all too limited resources. Other strategies are available and one approach is target setting.

Target setting

Target setting is very much at the forefront of current thinking and no serious work in school/nursery development is complete without a section on this approach, which is to become compulsory for all maintained schools from 1999. Targets for attainment originated from the National Curriculum, programmes of study that aimed to 'set demanding but achievable targets for what pupils of different ages should know, understand and be able to do'. Not surprisingly, many of these ideas have been translated to fit expectations for teachers, whether newly qualified or experienced. Specific, Measurable, Achievable, Realistic and Time-related provide good material for the acronym SMART but often fail to address the more complex issues of motivation. Drucker (1990) refers to man-

Stage	Task needs	Possible tasks
Exploration	1 Varied job activities 2 Self-exploration	
Establishment	1 Job challenge 2 Develop competence in a speciality area 3 Develop creativity and innovation 4 Rotate into new area after three to five years	
Mid career	1 Technical updating 2 Develop skills in training and coaching others (younger employees) 3 Rotation into new jobs requiring new skills 4 Develop broader view of work and own role in organisation	
Late career	1 Plan for retirement 2 Shift from power role to one of consultation and guidance 3 Identify and develop successors 4 Begin activities outside the organisation	

Figure 4.1 Training needs within career stages

agement by objectives (MBO) – it works if you know the objectives but 90 per cent of the time you don't. Target setting for staff therefore needs to be treated with similar caution.

Carol decided that setting individual performance targets would not be the most effective way of motivating staff at Cedars and Ashes. Setting goals in production situations can be beneficial, although where one person's performance depends upon the efforts of others it is difficult to assess an individual worker's contribution. In nurseries and schools such an approach would be inappropriate. Other concerns are the possible narrowness of goals which, in a nursery or school setting, could lead to tunnel vision, or the achievement of targets set at the expense of areas less easily measured, but just as important. In a nursery this might affect the quality of play or social time that staff arranged. Goals might be misinterpreted and, particularly in work with young children, there would be a danger that corners might be cut to achieve targets.

Carol believes that everyone needs to share in a vision based on 'customer' feedback.

The Deming approach

In reviewing current working patterns, Carol could turn to the philosophy of the late Dr W. Edward Deming whose thoughts on intrinsic motivation, self-esteem, dignity and security provide a stark contrast to current short-term target setting.

Deming's joiner triangle (Figure 4.2) is the starting-point to develop a programme of improvement for everyone. Deming's idea was based on three assumptions, which are:

1   That customers must get *what they want* and that quality begins with delighting the customer. Thus, in a nursery it is most important to provide quality education, not just to satisfy parents, but to delight them. This can only be achieved by studying what is currently being undertaken and assessing how it can be improved.
2   Variations exist, particularly when working with young children. A scientific approach of collecting data on records and assessments would help to see what could be improved and how much variation was acceptable in terms of attainment.
3   Cooperation is needed between individuals to become all one team (see chapter 3).

If she were to use this approach, Carol could begin by inviting staff to feed back their concerns regarding the nurseries, with her acting as a facilitator. She could confirm her 'impressions checking' by holding one-to-one conversations during her visits to the nurseries. However, for those who find it difficult to articulate their feelings a simple diagram allows everyone to confirm what they feel.

Carol could use three questions and staff could indicate their responses, as illustrated in Figures 4.3, 4.4, 4.5 and 4.6.

Figure 4.2 Deming's joiner triangle
Source: Neave 1990

The first question is:

1   How informed and up to date do you feel about developments? Please shade
    the circle (Figure 4.3).

Once again, as in the team-building exercise in chapter 3, the emphasis is
placed on staff being asked to communicate rather than only coming forward
when things are going wrong.
    The second question is:

2   How much do you feel involved in the work of the nursery? (Figure 4.4)

Seeking feedback in this way helps managers to gain rapid visual clues about
the feelings of individuals in an organisation. What such diagrams can reveal
is the isolation of groups within organisations and the separation of individuals from groups – useful indicators of the way staff are feeling in relation to
their work.
    The third question then focuses on getting individuals to respond to the
following:

3   Where I believe I am and where I want to be (Figures 4.5 and 4.6).

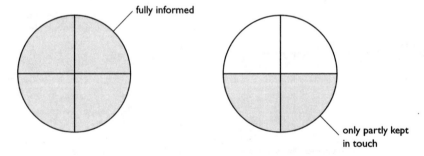

Figure 4.3 Staff feedback – feeling informed

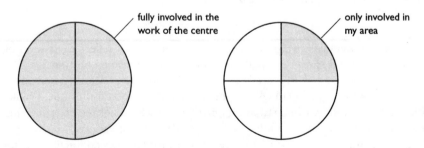

Figure 4.4 Staff feedback – feeling involved

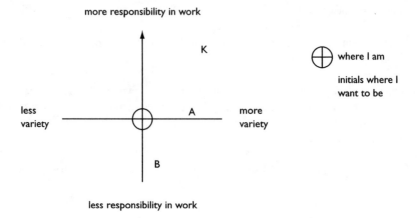

Figure 4.5 Level of responsibility matrix – example

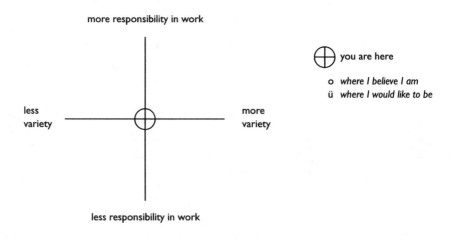

Figure 4.6 Level of responsibility matrix

Asking individuals to plot themselves on a matrix to reflect their level of responsibility and spread of work can provide the answer to question 3.

For example Kailash (K) seeks considerably more responsibility and more variety in her work. Abigail (A) is content with the responsibility but is looking for more variety. Brian (B) as an outreach worker is looking to reduce his responsibilities to schools while maintaining the level of variety.

Unfortunately, the three-pillar model of commitment does not include a cast-iron guarantee on obtaining commitment, something that industrial managers

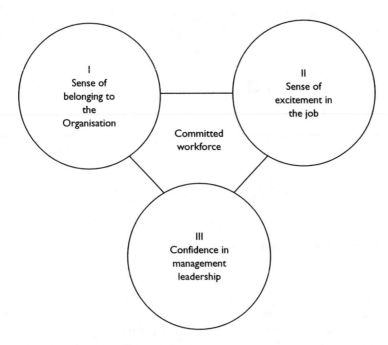

Figure 4.7 The three-pillar model of commitment
Source: Martin and Nicholls 1987: 27

REFLECTION (1)

How can a manager reduce the gap between o and ü in Figure 4.6 and thus increase the commitment of staff in order to create a committed workforce as Figure 4.7 shows?

---

learnt over fifty years ago, if the following quotation from Clarence Francis when he was chairman of General Foods is to be believed.

> You can buy a man's time; you can buy a man's physical presence at a given place; you can even buy a measured number of skilled muscular motions per hour or day; but you cannot buy enthusiasm. You cannot buy initiative; you cannot buy loyalty; you cannot buy devotion of hearts, minds, and souls. You have to earn these things.
>
> (Megginson, Mosley and Pietri 1986: 387)

Carol might find it useful to outline her programme with the Venn diagram in Figure 4.8, saying she sees every individual at the centre of the three circles.

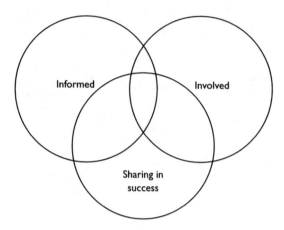

Figure 4.8 Venn diagram of staff motivation factors

This would enable her to increase motivation of staff by keeping them more informed and helping them to visualise future developments. Next she could seek the involvement of everyone, encouraging them to seek experience in different areas across the nursery. Only after participating in a broader range of work do people become aware of the needs and demands of customers. Third, she should be aware success comes through increased pride, along with trust and responsibility for setting realistic goals.

However, it remains Carol's job to initiate the entire process. Starting with paid staff is not enough – she must begin with the voluntary helpers whose roles do not yet appear on any analysis of jobs. Only by beginning the process of empowerment with those who have less of a stake in developments while at the same time demonstrating her openness to everyone will she get the responses she requires. Figure 4.9 is helpful when considering ways of empowering all stakeholders in order to achieve optimum motivation and greater satisfaction.

So far, this chapter has stressed the need for managers to take an active role in managing the motivation of workers. Responsibility rests with them to improve attitudes and participate fully in discussions. However, before becoming involved with others there is a need for self-examination. Managers should consider their own strengths and limitations, and the extent to which perceptions of themselves are shared by others. Next they need to recognise the individuality of every worker, particularly in a nursery or school setting where professionals and para-professionals demonstrate marked differences in needs, abilities and rewards. This has implications for the level of tasks and degree of challenge offered. Finally, if long-term success is to be achieved there needs to be increased trust, involvement and a sense of pride in all stakeholders.

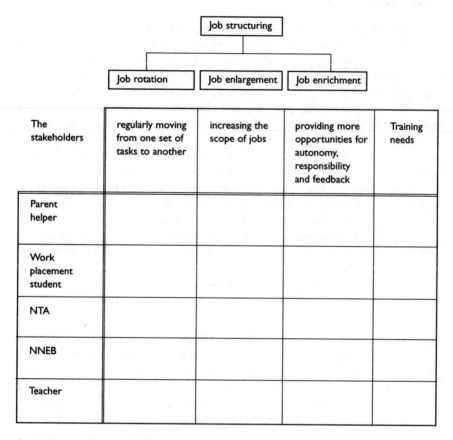

| Job structuring | | | |
| Job rotation | Job enlargement | Job enrichment | |

The stakeholders	regularly moving from one set of tasks to another	increasing the scope of jobs	providing more opportunities for autonomy, responsibility and feedback	Training needs
Parent helper				
Work placement student				
NTA				
NNEB				
Teacher				

Figure 4.9 Empowering stakeholders

ACTIVITY

Use Figure 4.9 to plan ways of enhancing the motivation of staff in your nursery or school. What conclusions can you make about

- job rotation?
- job enlargement?
- job enrichment?
- training needs?

Motivation and pay

No chapter on motivation would be complete without some comment on financial rewards. Pay is a sensitive issue in care and education and, despite the best intentions of the pay review bodies, looks likely to remain so. Any attempt to enhance some salaries in recognition of increased responsibilities runs counter to equity theory. This is the view that workers seek to maintain a fair balance between the rewards they get and the contribution they make, equal to the reward/contribution ratios of other workers with whom they compare themselves.

However, as Herzberg (1966) reminds us, salary still remains part of the maintenance package, one of those factors that needs to be 'kept clean' along with working conditions, policies and administration if the real motivators are to function properly. Exactly what these motivations are for professional people is a fascinating study in itself and one that regularly appears on the agenda of most education management courses. Despite being conducted over thirty years ago, Herzberg's conclusions about staff being 'switched on' by what their job involves and how they are recognised within their organisation remains remarkably similar today. Responsibilities and prospects, including the degree of security, all appear to play a part in the motivation package. Nevertheless, even if dissatisfaction itself is reduced, this alone will not motivate workers, as Figure 4.10 shows and Herzberg states.

> Five factors stand out as strong determiners of job satisfaction – achievement, recognition, work itself, responsibility and advancement – the last three being of greater importance for a lasting change of attitudes. These five factors appeared very infrequently when the respondents described events that paralleled job dissatisfaction feelings. A further word on recognition: when it appeared in a 'high' sequence of events, it referred to recognition for achievement rather than recognition as a human-relations tool divorced from any accomplishment. The latter type of recognition does not serve as a 'satisfier'.
>
> What is the explanation of such results? Do the two sets of factors have two separate themes: it appears so, for the factors on the right [in Figure 4.10] all seem to describe man's relationship to what he does; his job content, achievement on a task, recognition for task achievement, the nature of the task, responsibility for a task and professional advancement or growth in task capability.
>
> What is the central theme for the dissatisfiers? Restating the factors as the kind of administration and supervision received in doing the job, the nature of interpersonal relationships and working conditions that surround the job and the effect of salary suggest the distinction from the 'satisfiers' factors. Rather than describe man's relationship to what he does, the 'dissatisfier' factors describe his relationship to the context or environment in which he does his job. One cluster of factors relates to what the person does and the other to the situation in which he does it.

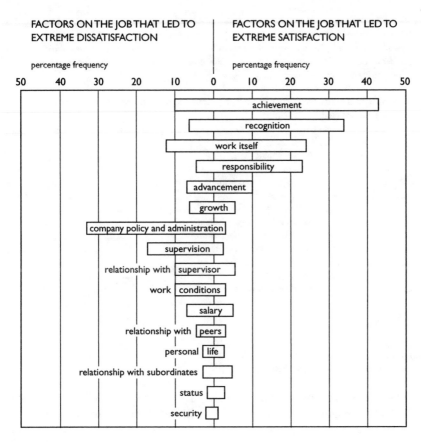

Figure 4.10 Factors of job satisfaction
Source: Herzberg 1966

Since the dissatisfier factors essentially describe the environment and serve primarily to prevent job dissatisfaction, while having little effect on positive job attitudes, they have been named the hygiene factors. This is an analogy to the medical use of the term meaning 'preventative and environmental'. Another term for these factors in current use is maintenance factors. The 'satisfier' factors were named the motivators, since the other findings of the study suggest that they are effective in motivating the individual to superior performance and effort.

(Herzberg 1966)

Working with teachers over the last ten years, we have designed Figure 4.11 to help them consider their own motivators and those of fellow workers. Complete Figure 4.11 yourself to identify what motivates you.

Our experiences with teachers have confirmed our view that Herzberg's

Below is a list of factors that may affect people's attitudes to their work. Please consider a 'typical' member of your staff and award them 5 points next to the category *they would consider* as being *the most important to them*. Give 4 points to the next most important and so on, leaving the rest blank.

When you have noted the factors important to staff, complete the second column in the same way for yourself.

Staff		*You*
....	Advancement	....
....	Achievement	....
....	School policy and Administration	....
....	Job interest	....
....	Personal relationships with colleagues	....
....	Personal life (factors outside work)	....
....	Recognition for effective work	....
....	Status and responsibility	....
....	Salary	....
....	Security	....
....	Working conditions	....
total 15		total 15

Figure 4.11 Needs and motivation
Source: Adapted from Herzberg 1966

theories still remain remarkably relevant to workers today. Achievement, job interest and recognition regularly score highly while status and responsibility and salary naturally remain important. The challenge for any leader is to enrich the job, and maintain the satisfaction both through feedback and the use of varied projects which can maintain that will to want to continue to do something well.

REFLECTION (2)

As a manager audit yourself:

- *Achievement*   *What opportunities have I provided for staff to contribute new ideas and develop their capabilities?*
- *Job interest*   *In what ways have I stressed the importance of the work of every member of staff?*
- *Recognition*   *How often do I provide feedback about staff performance?*
- *Status*   *How can I ensure the status and responsibility of staff is recognised and valued?*

Further reading

We have again selected three texts for discussion in this section, the first of which is *The Deming Dimension* (1990) **Henry Neave**. The book introduces the reader to the man credited as the architect of post-war Japanese industrial success. Deming's writings now form much of the basis of the Total Quality Management movement and are slowly being adapted by schools and others in education.

Neave begins with a biography of Dr Deming that helps to set his achievements in perspective, before moving to the famous 14 points and 'obsession with quality' statements. Understandably, these two statements lie at the heart of Deming's philosophy:

> Quality Guideline 1: Quality Begins with Delighting the Customer
> Customers must get what they want, when they want it, and how they want it. An organisation must strive not only to satisfy the customers' expectations. This is the least one should do. A company should also strive to delight their customers, giving them even more than they imagined possible. Your bosses may be ecstatic, the Board of Directors blissful, and your company may be considered a legend on Wall Street. But if your customers are not delighted, you have not begun to achieve quality.
>
> (Neave 1990: 32)

The 14 points developed over twenty years by Deming need to be understood in terms of the joiner triangle (see Figure 4.2).

1   Create constancy of purpose toward improvement of product and service, with the aim to become competitive and to stay in business, and to provide jobs.
2   Adopt the new philosophy. We are in a new economic and educational age. Early years educators along with other managers learn their responsibilities, and take on leadership for change.
3   Cease dependence on inspection to achieve quality. Eliminate the need for inspection on a mass basis by building quality into our work in the first place.
4   End the practice of awarding business on the basis of price tag. Instead, minimise total cost. Move toward a single supplier for any one item, on a long-term relationship of loyalty and trust.
5   Improve constantly and forever the system of production and service, to improve quality and productivity, and thus constantly to decrease costs.
6   Institute training on the job.
7   Institute leadership (see point 12). The aim of leadership should be to help people and machines and gadgets to do a better job.

Leadership of management is in need of overhaul, as well as leadership of production workers.

8   Drive out fear, so that everyone may work effectively for the company.
9   Break down barriers between departments. People in research, design, sales, and production must be in touch with the product or service.
10   Eliminate slogans, exhortations, and targets for the work force asking for zero defects and new levels of productivity.
11a   Eliminate work standards (quotas) on the factory floor. Substitute leadership.
  b   Eliminate management by objective.
      Eliminate management by numbers, numerical goals. Substitute leadership.
12a   Remove barriers that rob the hourly worker of her or his right to pride of workmanship. The responsibility of supervisors must be changed from sheer numbers to quality.
  b   Remove barriers that rob people in management and in engineering of their right to pride of workmanship. This means, inter alia, abolishment of the annual or merit rating and of management by objective, management by the numbers.

(Deming 1986: 23–4)

Not surprisingly, various attempts have been made to align these points more towards education, the most notable adaptation being that of Greenwood and Gaunt (1994: 148).

Deming's 14 points adapted for schools

1   Pursue continuous improvement of curriculum and learning diligently and constantly.
2   Adopt the system of profound knowledge in your classroom and school as the prime management tool.
3   Build quality into teaching and learning and reduce the inspection of quality into work after the event.
4   Build a partnership relationship with colleagues, students, parents, colleges and employers.
5   Constantly improve the system within which teaching/learning takes place.
6   Take every opportunity to train in new skills and to learn from your pupils.
7   Lead, do not drive or manipulate.
8   Drive out fear of punishment, create joy in learning.
9   Collaborate with colleagues from other departments and functions.
10   Communicate honestly, not through jargon and slogans.
11   As far as possible create a world without grades and rank orders.
12   Encourage and celebrate to develop your student's pride in work.

13 Promote the development of the whole person in students and colleagues.
14 Wed your students to learning by the negotiation with them of a quality experience.

Also discussed in considerable detail are Deming's views on what he termed the 'Deadly Diseases'.

1 Lack of constancy – another barrier to continuous improvement.
2 Short-termism – a similarly misplaced viewpoint.
3 Job hopping – the mobility of management that he felt brought instability and offered only irrelevant experience gained elsewhere. However, it was performance appraisal that Deming reserved for his fiercest criticisms.

Part two of the book develops the fundamentals of Deming's philosophy, beginning with two experiments he instituted to demonstrate the nature of variation and learning about management thinking. The Funnel Experiment and the Red Beads sampling provide evidence of the nature of variation with messages more relevant to education than would at first be thought. Deming demonstrated that variation occurs whether in manufacturing or education. As educators we cannot expect targets to be achieved all the time by every class or group. Each young child is an individual who brings a range of experience and attitudes. Simply to subject them to relentless testing and targeting is to misunderstand the whole process of education and the role of management within it. Chapters on cooperation, 'win win' as the new philosophy, joy in work and innovation, not just improvement, illustrate the 'profound knowledge' and belief that 'everybody could gain over the long term' with a little more psychology to remind us.

Psychology helps us to understand (predict) how uncertainty and variation in circumstances affect people. Circumstances will affect people in different ways. The interaction of any person with circumstances may vary rapidly with time. The reward system in a company is an example of circumstances; the management is another and a transformation in government, industry and education.

Our second recommendation is **Motivation and Work Behaviour** (1983) **Richard Steers and Lyman Porter**. This text provides an encyclopaedic account of knowledge of motivation in the workplace together with a historical perspective and critical comment. Major theories are analysed and supplemented by further comment and discussion questions. Part one opens with some basic considerations of the motivation process, drive and reinforcement theories, expectations and valence (values) of outcomes, before considering managerial approaches to motivation in terms of assumptions, policies and expectations.

Part two considers the 'need' theories, beginning with Maslow and amended by Murray, to consider achievement, and affiliation needs, autonomy and power together with their implications for a manager. Cognitive theories of motivation in relation to goal setting and equity are examined along with explanations about the value of reinforcement and its underlying assumptions.

Motivation at work and the reward systems of organisations are discussed in the context of politics, war, medicine and universities as well as business, with 'How to ruin motivation with pay' providing a fitting end to an enlightening chapter. The punishment and sanction chapter is followed by one on job attitude, stress and performance that contains some valuable data on predicting performance, attitude and arousal and coping strategies. Social influences on motivation as part of group pressure and group performance are discussed as part of the complex process variables that exist within organisations.

Employee attitudes and commitment are defined as 'part of the process in which an individual identifies with an organisation and its goals and so becomes increasingly integrated or congruent'. This proves an interesting area with considerable implications for a manager, as well as providing a useful guide to employee attendance and voluntary turnover (p. 473).

The final chapters on job design and quality of work provide further insights into job characteristics as a means of work motivation through greater enrichment, variety and feedback from clients. These are designed to increase quality of work-life improvements while at the same time taking account of cultural influences that affect motivation and performance.

Our third recommended book is *Management and Motivation* (1970) **edited by Victor Vroom and Edward Deci.** This is a collection of writings beginning with a section on why men (*sic*) work. Here Simons (1947) writes about inducements and incentives for employees from a somewhat dated perspective. Maslow's famous theories follow to provide a detailed discussion, despite it being more than fifty years since their initial publication. The last chapter in this section considers the function and meaning of work through tables of statistics that are again of limited value given their 1950s research base.

Part two – on satisfaction – begins with the consequences of job satisfaction and the relationship to turnover, while a second article casts doubt on the relationship between satisfaction and job performance in relation to industrial workers. Herzberg's famous study on job satisfaction (achievement, recognition, work itself, responsibility and advancement) and the subsequent explanation of 'duality regarding job attitudes' is the next key chapter. Likewise Vroom (1969) and March and Simon (1958) consider variables that determine attitudes towards participation and the subsequent movement of staff within and between organisations.

Part three considers specific aspects of the work environment, beginning with financial inducements including sections on performance and pay, secret pay policies, compensation policies and pay preferences. Later in this section, Tannenbaum provides a chapter on the group in organisations and links aspects of group pressure and conformity to motivation and productivity. Daniel Katz discusses motivational patterns that can be employed in 'organisational settings' together with the consequences and conditions in relation to role performance. Frederick Taylor's writings on the principles of scientific management as seen through the selection, training, teaching and developing of workers in conjunction with management and as an equal division of tasks is discussed in relation to bonuses and premiums. McGregor's theory X or Y as part of the 'human side of enterprise' completes an authoritative chapter. The final sections concentrate on the human aspects of organisations and how participative beliefs retain a strong value element that includes a 'happiness factor' which in turn can lead to increased innovation and flexibility.

The contributions from such well-known writers together with other supporting theories provide an important resource for any manager as well as confirming the complexity and range of motivation behaviour in the work place.

Chapter 5

Managing the challenge of change

This chapter focuses on: The skills needed to manage change
Guidelines for successful change
Dealing with resistance

with examples of how change can be achieved successfully and integrated
into people's working patterns.

We look at the process of change and individuals' responses to change within
organisations. We consider some of the strategies managers can adopt, as well
as the skills managers need, in effecting successful change. We then examine
the reasons why change is viewed both positively and negatively by different
people; how resistance to change can be both identified and overcome and the
ways in which it can be negotiated.

In order to address the challenge of change, the reader is asked to consider
a school's response to falling attendance rolls in a changing political climate in
which providers of education for under 5s are required to work in partnership.
The case study focuses on teachers who are unused to working alongside voluntary groups and who experience problems in adjusting to the changes. It
considers the options available to Beth, Coordinator for Early Years, in developing the school's community involvement, changing its role with other agencies and taking the staff along with her in welcoming the changes.

Throughout the chapter there are opportunities for the reader to consider
her or his own response to change in order to begin to understand why others
respond to it in the myriad ways they do.

**Look at the school layout plus staff and their roles before reading the case
study. Begin to identify for yourself the difficulties that will be encountered in bringing about a positive solution to what is currently a problem.**

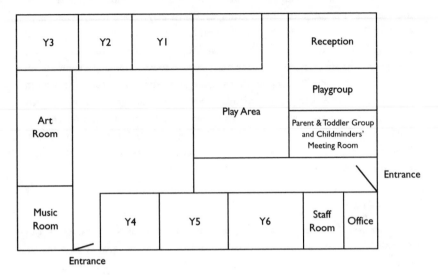

Figure 5.1 Damson Lane Primary School

Table 5.1 Members of staff involved

Name	Role
Beth	Early Years co-ordinator
Rosemary	Reception teacher
Delia	Nursery nurse

CASE STUDY

The school and the community

Damson Lane Primary School is a 1960s 'new' building in need of renovation. There are several empty classrooms and the jobs of staff are at considerable risk because they have been unable to attract families to the school. Class numbers are falling.

After extensive research in the area and a great deal of networking it has become clear that the space within the school, resulting from falling rolls, can be viewed as an advantage since it allows them to consider developing the school, both for, and with, the community. The Senior Management Team, together with the help of the governing body, envisage it as a centre of excellence. However, they are aware that there must be dramatic changes if they are to compete effectively with other nearby schools which enjoy a better reputation.

The community is mixed and while there is much deprivation in some areas, there is also a prestigious new housing estate nearby where many young families live. There is an elderly persons' home next to the school and a social services family centre nearby. In addition, the newly built health centre and a new parade of shops make it a busy place where many people are likely to be.

As a result of preliminary work, the playgroup has asked to be housed in one of the empty classrooms and this request has been granted. This has led some parents to ask whether they can have premises to set up a parent and toddler group and local childminders have also asked for a meeting room. Parents, particularly in the winter months, have also asked for use of a room so that they can meet from time to time.

The issues

The success of the proposed changes is apparent to all who recognise the valuable role that can be played by schools in developing as a community resource. However, the reception teacher and the nursery nurse feel particularly aggrieved about the way the process has progressed.

They argue that their work is being made more difficult because there are now three rooms near their classroom which are used, in Rosemary's words, by 'anybody and everybody'. They also feel undervalued because they believe that their professionalism is being threatened by the Senior Management Team (SMT)'s decision to allow untrained workers in the school to work with young children. They believe this indicates the SMT's belief that the work in the reception class is more like childminding than teaching. A third issue is their concern about the way these 'untrained' people manage children. They state that children are often uncontrolled and that the workers don't maintain the required safety procedures such as keeping children in view at all times and locking external doors.

Beth, whose role is to manage the change, has a great deal of work to do in order to prevent the hostility of Rosemary the teacher, and Delia the nursery nurse from becoming more than 'murmuring' about it. Equally she is charged with taking more far-reaching changes forward so she must succeed in convincing them that the change is worthwhile. She realises that there may be some truth in what the teacher and the nursery nurse are concerned about but she considers the biggest difficulty is related to the way the staff are choosing to look at what is happening.

As Andrew Leigh notes in his book *Effective Change* (1994), there are no levers of change to pull which will always work or are foolproof in every situation and, given the diverse nature of nurseries and schools, this is hardly surprising. Instead there are certain skills needed by managers, some of which can be seen in Figure 5.2. Analysing these skills should help Beth to become aware of how she should develop her own skills in order to help her colleagues.

Pedler *et al.* (1978) believe that every manager needs to 'become familiar with the effects of change on themselves and other people'. They stress the need to be concerned with planning change and anticipating its effects. They also suggest that people intent on bringing about change (change agents) should begin by thinking about their own reaction to change. They should consider how they feel, or would feel if somebody moved the furniture in their office or home, or how they would feel about having to wear a particular style of clothing for work. When individuals honestly review their own response to change they may realise that imposed change can feel uncomfortable. They suggest that every change agent should begin by reviewing their own experiences.

ACTIVITY

Identify two recent changes in your work or personal circumstances and say whether you welcomed or questioned the change.

REFLECTION (1)

How do you respond to change?

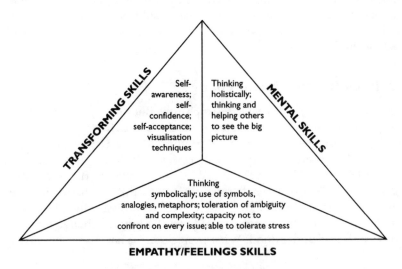

Figure 5.2 New skills managers need for handling change
Source: Adapted from Leigh 1994

One thing is certain – while there is no one definitive model there are nevertheless a few basic principles and preparatory activities that can help any change agent faced with a similar task to Beth's. The first task must be to **build the right relationship with the people who are going to be participants,** which Havelock (1973) compares to a fragile bridge: 'A good relationship is a complex and delicate bridge, very difficult and expensive to build and very important to maintain'.

Although there is no formula, seven common characteristics comprise an ideal base for Beth or anyone else embarking on an effective change programme. These are:

1   **Reciprocity** – all parties should be able to give and take. Understanding the problem from another angle helps diagnosis and increases transfer of information.
2   **Openness** – both parties need to receive inputs from each other, including feedback and new ideas.
3   **Realistic expectations** – both of others and yourself. Try to counteract any impressions of enormous benefits by not overselling yourself or the project.
4   **Expectations of reward** – some token of future reward is necessary as evidence of help and success, for example more opportunities for staff for variety or responsibility.
5   **Structure** – it is important that roles and relationships are as clearly defined as working procedures.
6   **Minimum threat** – disturbances rather than benefits are often seen as the outcome. Any change must actively seek to minimise such a perception.
7   **Involvement of all parties** – everyone should be able to be involved although the programme will inevitably make some demands of individuals at different stages.

Guidelines for successful change

It is generally believed that people resist change. But do they? Does a teacher or nursery nurse resist an allowance for work she is already covering? Does an ancillary refuse payment for extra responsibility? Does a Head reject an offer to represent the school at an important reception? All these changes are likely to be warmly welcomed and met with cooperation. What distinguishes these changes from the ones that people resist strongly is the fact that their nature and effects are relatively well known and received enthusiastically. **The degree of people's resistance to change depends on the kind of change involved and how well it is understood.** What people resist is not change but loss, or the possibility of loss.

In bringing about change, Beth and her managers should be sensitive to the feelings of the reception and nursery teachers who may not feel that they have

REFLECTION (2)

Last time you led or participated in a change programme how many of the forces in Figure 5.3 were in evidence? Use the figure to examine each of the forces and note down evidence of each.

			Evidence
1	Reciprocity	Did you or the change agent try to see the issue from the other side?	
2	Openness	How receptive were people to feedback and modification?	
3	Realistic expectations	Was there evidence of 'hype' by people that was unwarranted?	
4	Rewards	Were these made clear if any existed?	
5	Structure	How much time was taken in establishing ground rules?	
6	Threats	How were these handled and minimised?	
7	Involvement	What attempts were made to take and keep everyone on board?	

Figure 5.3 Change programme checklist

What have you found out? Which characteristics were apparent – all, most, some? What does this suggest about the way the programme was developed?

any say in the ongoing changes in the school which inevitably affect their own roles and working conditions.

This chapter has focused on approaches and mechanisms but change, like every other aspect of management, requires the involvement of people, and that in turn can result in unpredictable reactions and differing behaviours. Although you may be able to anticipate some of the responses, nothing can ever be certain, nor will it remain static. In this sense timing and luck always play a part. However, the positive manager can always use the current circumstances to maximum advantage rather than blaming events and people. That there is no one prescription does not mean that there are not certain guidelines that can help to decide any course of action. The change agent should endeavour to do the following:

1   **Keep the information short and simple**
    The more technical it becomes, the more the person affected by change feels resistant. Their response can often be to ask for more technical information until they feel satisfied. Rather than sharing issues, a barrier has been created that can often result in 'nit picking' until the impact of new ideas has been lost.

2   **Focus on direction**
    The more you can promote tolerance of the need to move and test approaches, the more involved people will feel. Staff will be more motivated if they feel they can join in rather than being 'pushed under' straight away.

3   **Build on training**
    If previous experiences in other centres or schools is drawn upon then staff confidence in their own abilities increases. However a clear recognition of the time invested is necessary to familiarise and train people in a non-threatening environment.

4   **Create a culture of self-renewal**
    When you have gone there will be a return to the old ways. Build in an understanding through discussion and example that change is on the agenda and that help exists from outside, as well as providing people with the skills to diagnose what is needed from within.

5   **Audit yourself**
    Have you got the skills and credibility to effect change? Are you perceived by staff as someone who simply wants to impress others or further their own ends? Do staff feel threatened? Are the benefits and rewards obvious?

Looking back to the case study it is evident that the two teachers who are hostile to the changes are uncertain about the way the changes will affect them. Their uncertainties are:

*   they feel that the work they do as teachers is being undervalued;
*   they feel it difficult to accept that they should work alongside 'non-teachers';
*   others rather than themselves are responsible for some of the children in the building who seem 'out of control';
*   some people don't seem to understand the safety policy/procedure in school.

Responses to change

Figure 5.4 reflects most people's thinking. Can you locate how the teachers in the case study have responded to the change?

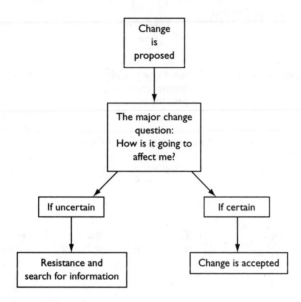

Figure 5.4 Responses to change

Writers on change strategies distinguish between collaborative and coercive approaches. Within the school or nursery setting there is little place for coercion:

1   Coercion leads to strong efforts to avoid being coerced.
2   If resources for fighting back are available, the greater the coercion applied the more counter aggression is called forth.
3   If resources are not available but opportunities to escape are, the greater the tendency to leave the situation.
4   If resources for fighting back and opportunities to escape are not available, or if there are other strong incentives for staying in the situation (material rewards or potential power), the greater coercion that is applied the greater the tendency to comply with exactly those demands that are necessary to avoid being coerced. In other words, just doing enough but no more to keep management off your back.
5   If resources for fighting back and opportunities for escape are not available, the . . . tendency to dull compliance and passive resistance [is increased].

(Owens 1987: 254)

Such views have considerable implications for Beth and reinforce the need for clear action steps which she must take if the planned changes are to be successful. Table 5.2 provides a framework on which she could base her actions.

Table 5.2 Action steps framework

Implication		Action steps		Possible strategies
Need to motivate change	1	Identify any surface dissatisfaction with the present state	1	Hold a meeting with the teachers; all groups together
	2	Participation in change	2	Involve them in planning
	3	Rewards for behaviour in support of change	3	Offer responsibility points if available
	4	Time and opportunity to disengage from the present state	4	Accept they need time to think – giving this helps them not to lose 'face'
Need to manage the transition	5	Develop and communicate a clear image of the future	5	Involve staff in visiting other centres and defining what they would like to see; visit other successful community schools
	6	Use multiple and consistent leverage points		
	7	Develop organisational arrangements for the transition		
	8	Build in feedback mechanisms		
Need to shape the political dynamics of change	9	Assure the support of key power groups	9	E.g. governors, senior management team
	10	Use leader behaviour to generate energy in support of change	10	Show that you are enthusiastic and positive about the change yourself
	11	Use symbols and language		
	12	Build in stability		

Source: Adapted from Dalin and Rust 1983

Gaining acceptance of change

In order for change to be accepted and fully integrated, the group barriers which maintain the status quo need to be diagnosed carefully. Barriers are created by different responses to change.

Three types of people play a significant part in generating group acceptance. These are the 'innovators', the 'resisters', and the 'leaders'. Because the characteristics of these three types of people have been studied extensively by social scientists, we are in a position to understand who they are and how they work regardless of the particular innovation we are concerned with.

(Havelock 1973: 119)

Types

- **Innovators** tend to be risk takers and are often prepared to risk sticking their neck out over new ideas.
- **Resisters** see themselves as defenders of the current system whose job is to preserve the status quo and often prevent new influences.
- **Leaders** are the influential people who often watch carefully before committing themselves to any innovation.

REFLECTION (3)

Which groups can you identify in the case study? How can Beth change attitudes?

Although general, these categories can nevertheless often help a manager decide whom to target with any new venture. Beginning to get the innovators on board first and persuading them to demonstrate the positive aspects of the change to others can lead to resisters having many of their concerns neutralised. Finally, leaders' will be influenced and commit themselves to the proposed changes.

Once this has been achieved there is still a place for continuing reward and reinforcement together with practice and evaluation as a basis for building on self-renewal among staff.

Dealing with resistance

Resistance can take many forms and permutations. People are naturally wary, often because they perceive things to be out of their control.

Resistance to change can include:

- A desire not to lose something of value.
- A misunderstanding of the change and its implications.
- A belief that it doesn't make sense.
- A low tolerance for change – fear of not being able to develop new skills and behaviour required of them.

(Kotter *et al.* 1986)

Looking back at the case study we find some examples that Beth might employ to help her (Table 5.3).

Finally, it must be remembered that, as in all things, there will be winners and losers, benefits and costs, with each person calculating their personal cost-benefit analysis as 'Responses to change'.

Watson makes two key points in his paper 'The loser and the management of change' (1986). First, an 'abort button' should be built into the planning stage; if the change does not meet certain conditions over a period of time it should be amended or discontinued. Second, one of the head teacher's or manager's special responsibilities should be to 'minimize the costs to the losers, rather than maximise the benefits to the gainers'. If these two conditions are observed then the chances of success will be greatly increased.

So, Beth and other managers need to be aware of the need to be flexible in their approach to change and should work to make sure the benefits of the change outweigh the costs.

Table 5.3   Dealing with resistance

Examples	Interpretation	Possible solutions
The work of the teachers is undervalued; Unwilling to work alongside 'non-teachers'.	Misunderstandings, selective perception, self interest	Finding positive ways of reducing fear – meetings, sharing expertise, resources, views
Recommendations and/or pledges about resourcing were not kept.	Legacy of previous change and ensuring lack of trust	Record everything and ensure people are familiar with procedures
A short-term solution to satisfy immediate demands.	The quick fix	Keep staff informed and ask them to look ahead
Things were better when they knew what was going on.	Security in the past	Getting them involved in any future plans
Uncertainties about roles leave them concerned about Health and Safety issues.	Ill-prepared staff	Devise shared policies and procedures
They may be concerned that their own roles will change whether they like it or not – they may worry about becoming 'childminders'.	Threats to power of freedom	INSET focused on the concept of partnership, continuity of experience and the importance of transition for young children

Further reading

In our discussions of change we first selected *The Change Agent's Guide to Innovation in Education* (1973) Ronald Havelock which describes itself as a guide to the process of innovation, providing information on 'how successful innovation takes place and how change agents can organize their work to effect it'. The guide offers advice on planning, ideas and checklists, as well as things to avoid, plus guidelines on well-proven tactics based on over 1,000 studies of schools and centres. The role of the change agent is summarised in four areas as shown in Figure 5.5, which illustrates how each one fits into the change process. Although the guide stresses that roles are not mutually exclusive, the example of a process helper is taken as an illustration for the six main sections of the book.

Stage I – *Relationship* emphasises the need to relate to the client. Questions such as what are the normal beliefs, boundaries and values? Who are the leaders, influencers and gatekeepers? (those who control channels of influence) all provide a useful starting-point towards examining the relationship established with colleagues, whether that is someone working from the inside or an external consultant.

Stage II – *Diagnosis* provides advice on understanding current problems and identifying opportunities in the context of the current situation, leading to a checklist of goals, capacity, structure and rewards.

Stage III – champions the *need for resources* to diagnose, survey, pilot, evaluate, install and maintain any innovation and so underlines the importance of acquiring and achieving the necessary levels of provision.

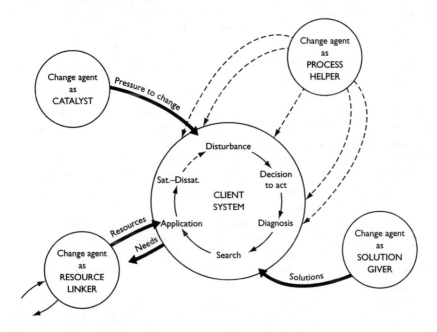

Figure 5.5 Four ways to be a change agent
Source: Havelock 1973

Stage IV – is concerned with *choosing and generating a range of ideas*, their feasibility and possible adoption.

Stage V – *Gaining acceptance* is concerned with the process of adopting an innovation. Starting with an individual's awareness and passive interest, the initial encounters may well influence subsequent motivation. The interest stage is characterised by more active information that leads to the development of positive or negative attitudes. Further evaluation by the individual is in terms of whether she or he should make the effort that leads to a trial and, on the basis of favourable results, acceptance. However, as Havelock states, 'true adoption cannot be considered to have taken place unless the innovation becomes routine. It must be integrated into the day to day working life of the teacher (or nursery officer).'

Stage VI – Many an innovation is superficially accepted, yet months or years later things drift back. Havelock advocates continuing reward, practice, provision of time and money, evaluation, maintenance and adoption as a *basis for self renewal*.

While all these ideas are workable the inclusion of case studies and quotations alongside the text provides a further practical focus and additional element for an already valuable resource.

In **Can Schools Learn** (1983) **Per Dalin and Val Rust** a framework for school improvement and institutional development is outlined that has been in use for several years and could be adapted to other settings. Chapter 1 begins with the premise that if the individual school is the key organisational unit of formal education then it should also be the basic unit for educational development and the primary force for change. The degree to which this applies is a combination of organisational creativity and adaptation to political, economic and environmental circumstances.

Organisational development (OD) is traced from its origins in the social and behavioural sciences and defined as a 'holistic attempt to improve the health and functioning of schools'. OD is seen as a self-correcting, self-renewing process with group members identifying the strengths and weaknesses (often with the aid of consultants) as part of a deliberate long-term process that involves self-assessment, problem solving and indication. Despite its apparent complexity, project evolutions from the United States reflect an overwhelming acceptance of the process.

The ten-step programme a school undertakes as part of an Institutional Development Programme is outlined graphically and, together with a guide to institutional learning about the ways in which schools confront problems (both actual and ideal), provides an important source of data for proposed improvement that can guide future discussion.

Obstacles in school development leads to a section on networking and evaluation that is supported by five case studies and commentaries. Lessons learnt from these projects across Europe and the US ensure a detailed analysis that includes views from head teachers and consultants. The final section focuses on the inevitable dilemmas between the individual and the organisation, process versus content and leaders against staff but remains committed to OD as a change strategy in schools.

> Finally, we are still committed to OD as a change strategy in schools. We know it can work. At the same time, we are also convinced that the OD process is a major innovation in its own right, difficult to implement, and hard to evaluate. We know that the more we gain insights into schools as organizations, the more we shall be able to master the complex process of school renewal.
>
> (Dalin and Rust 1983: 178)

Our last book, *A Strategy of Change* (1992) **David Wilson**, endeavours to 'provide some analytical perspectives on the understanding of organizational change' by focusing on planned and emergent change in the context of process and implementation. Underlying assumptions are considered within a framework of conflict and tension that provides the impetus for change along with the strategic choices identified by a manager scanning the environment to effect change. Collaboration or coercion as change processes are examined in relation to 'organisational fit' and the inevitable difficulties of diagnosing the environment over the last decade. However, despite North American and Japanese best practice being largely dominant in a spirit of the enterprise culture with increasing faith placed in consultants and change agents, there remains a certain caution by the author in a detailed assessment of economic practice.

Incremental change and the exercise of power is examined from a gender perspective as a basis for preserving the status quo; and is followed by the role of culture in organisations and the clues towards its interpretation, as well as the links with change, that inevitably exist. Programmed approaches, principally through Total Quality Management and its implications for management training, are considered to lead towards a set of competences.

Gaps between theory and practice in the management of change are identified in a final section that concludes that those with the loudest voices are often assumed to have the 'route to truth' in 'Change Management', but in fact such are the complexities of the process that to operate successfully she or he must 'learn from a wider context or organization' and so 'organize their own thoughts' without 'over-dependence on readily accessible models or seemingly powerful metaphors.'

Chapter 6

Communicating the vision

This chapter focuses on: Approaches to communication in nurseries and schools
The barriers to effective communication
Strategies to achieve improved communication

with examples of how a more effective communication system can be achieved.

In this chapter we explore the way in which communication is often taken for granted or left to chance and highlight the importance to schools and nurseries of effective ways of communicating. The case study examines both the factors that contribute to successful communication and create barriers to communication, and offers strategies for developing more successful communication between people. In the case study the reader is introduced to Elizabeth, a manager, who has an unpleasant message to communicate to staff. The illustrative material underlines the importance for managers of being clear about the messages they wish to convey and indicates some of the dangers and misperceptions that arise from getting the message wrong.

Nobody likes to be misunderstood. Everyone seeks to understand everyone else yet, despite years of practice and our best efforts, communication in the workplace is always an area for review and improvement. Part of the reason for this is a fundamental misunderstanding about the nature of communication. It is different from information, it makes demands and is based on perception and expectation. The following quotation can be found in staffrooms and workplaces all over the country.

I know you believe you understand what you think I said. But I am not sure you realise that what you heard is not what I meant.

People 'construct meanings and develop expectations through the exchange of symbols' (Myers and Myers 1982: 10). These symbols are highly personal and are based on individual experiences. When we wish to communicate we hope that the symbols we deploy create an experience similar to our own. We learn the impact of our messages by watching and observing the impact on others and so use these messages as a further guide to the process. Such a complicated explanation might appear unnecessary to describe the fact in the case study that Elizabeth failed to get her message across. The question is why? How can she ensure that next time she leaves everyone less dazed and confused and more aware that what they heard is what she meant?

CASE STUDY

Elizabeth is due to take over shortly as manager of a combined nursery centre, a result of the amalgamation on one site of two separate nurseries. This follows the local authority's commitment to integrated childcare and education for all children under 5. The local authority held a series of meetings with staff, warning them of the impending changes but most of the staff still feel upset, uncertain and in need of reassurance and support as they realise that not all of them will be fortunate enough to retain jobs in the amalgamation.

They have, therefore, asked for a meeting with Elizabeth so that they can discuss the problems of the amalgamation and clarify their perceptions of where the amalgamation will lead in terms of jobs. Elizabeth has agreed to the meeting at short notice, without seeking support and guidance from her own managers, because she feels fairly clear about the implications of the amalgamation. She knows it will mean that fewer staff will be required in the new nursery, Furzewood Children's Centre, than were previously employed on the two sites. She is therefore pleased to be able to meet the staff from both establishments at the new centre, after work has finished, so that she can 'clear things up' for them. In her haste to accommodate staff demands she has overlooked several important points. She has hurriedly gathered together the 'facts', although she is unsure of some of these; she has failed to set out a clear agenda and she has not notified all staff that the meeting is to take place. Neither has she thought about providing appropriate accommodation or refreshments for the meeting. For the seating arrangements she has adopted the 'Schoolroom' style (see Figure 6.1), with staff seated at children's tables and chairs.

REFLECTION (1)

Which seating arrangement would have been appropriate for this type of meeting?

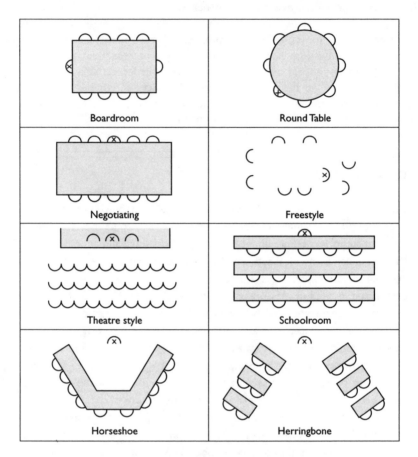

Figure 6.1 Seating arrangements for meetings (X = Chairperson)
Source: Peel 1990

In her anxiety to please staff, the meeting was so quickly organised that Elizabeth didn't have enough time to mentally translate the jargon into every-day language and as a result she did not inform staff of the 'facts'. So, rather than telling the staff how many job losses would occur, she talked about shed-ding staff; downsizing; natural wastage; redeployment; redundancy; short-term contracts and supply staff. Then she spoke very lengthily about future prospects before telling staff she could not make any promises regarding the future.

At first staff listened quietly but after a while there was a good deal of muttering to be heard, as people spoke to one another while she was talking. Elizabeth did not take any cues from her audience and seriously under-estimated the purpose of the meeting; she saw it as an information-giving exercise, whereas the staff had visualised an opportunity to exchange information. Because she talked and did not offer any opportunity for people to ask questions one of the longest serving members of staff, who had already decided to take early retirement, decided to act as spokesperson. She pointed out that Elizabeth was confusing them, was not talking straight and that the staff were more uncertain than ever of the consequences of the changes. She also told Elizabeth that the failure to provide them with a drink after a long day working with children showed that she did not understand the demands of their job. The meeting broke up in confusion and a lot of people were angry and resentful about the proposals.

Communication is perception

Elizabeth's use of words, symbols and actions were at odds with those of the staff and the result is that she failed to get her message across to them. We are not saying that Elizabeth did not communicate at all, for her silent language, that is her 'body language', would have made an impression upon staff without her speaking a single word. 'One cannot communicate a word; the whole (wo)man always comes with it' (Drucker 1979). Drucker goes on to make the point that people have to be spoken to in terms of their own experience and that the most important point is that the communication is within the receiver's range of understanding. A simple example of this is the ways in which we, as adults, adjust our language to young children, so that the message we want to get across to them is appropriate to their level of understanding. So we simplify what we have to say and in that way we manage to communicate quite complex ideas to young people.

Communication is expectation

Just as we see largely what we want to see, so we tend to hear what we want to hear. Our minds work within a frame of expectation and we learn to expect certain types of communication in particular situations. So, if we ring the telephone operator we don't expect her to ask us about ourselves, yet if we go to the doctor we do expect to be asked how we are. Confusion often arises from expecting certain types of interaction because we are in a particular setting and many experiments show that our behaviour is affected by our expectations.

So, if we want people to take notice of anything new or different that we wish to communicate, we need to prepare them for it by signposting or 'flagging' up to them what we will be saying. We use this approach all the time with young children when we prepare them for things throughout the day. For example, we may say to a group of children 'In a few minutes it will be time to tidy away' and then we may say 'Do you remember, we said it was soon going to be time to tidy up, well we need to begin tidying away now'. In other words we signal our intention to the listener. It is therefore important when we communicate that we prepare people by giving them things to listen out for. Elizabeth might have told her audience that she was going to speak about three things:

1   Numbers of staff
2   Number of jobs available
3   Alternative employment

In this way she would have made clear for herself and the staff the most important aspects of what she planned to talk about, and when she had finished talking both she and they could have checked to see she had addressed each area fully. Small steps like this help to prepare the listener for hearing what the speaker wishes to communicate.

Communication makes demands

Communication makes demands on both the speaker and the listener and 'people skills' need to be practised, preferably away from the workplace. Everybody, especially managers, should be aware of their own skills as communicators and ideally they should be able to see and hear their own performance as well as receive constructive feedback about it. Managers need to be able to project into the reality of their staff's experiences in order to imagine how they are feeling and how they will respond to what is being said at a particular time. In other words, managers should be aware that staff may choose not to listen if the message is communicated inappropriately. This also includes feelings that the time or the place is inappropriate.

In the case study Elizabeth delivered the news to staff who had been working with children all day and whose work with children demanded a very different frame of reference from that required in a meeting. Staff were therefore not prepared for the demands made upon them in the meeting and were not given the opportunity to move into what has been described as a 'zone of receivership'. In other words when the conditions are appropriate and staff are prepared they are in a 'zone of receivership' and are much more likely to hear the message that is being communicated.

You may wonder, at this point, how any successful communication takes place at all. Indeed, given the complexities and the demands made upon staff it is a tribute to their powers of concentration that so few misunderstandings occur. Nevertheless, barriers to communication exist in all settings, even in nurseries and schools, so it is important to be aware of their existence and proactive in finding ways to eradicate them. Table 6.1 shows some of the problems encountered in communication together with possible ways to overcome these. All of these solutions require a high degree of skill on the part of the manager.

Every manager needs to develop good communication skills, indeed

Table 6.1 Solutions to potential communication problems

Problems in school/nursery communication skills		Possible solutions
DISTANCE	Consider the distance the information has to travel and whether this problem is linked with a lack of face-to-face communication.	Establish a programme of meetings with agreed agendas that include one part of a staff training day for major items.
DISTORTION	It may be difficult to separate facts from perceptions and prejudices which can arise over distance.	Provide staff with briefing sheets of headings following meetings.
LACK OF HONESTY	People feel that they cannot level with superiors or subordinates.	Consider opportunities for informal feedback.
LACK OF TRUST	If previous communication experiences have been difficult for an individual, then the situation is unlikely to be repeated.	Check the impression you are making. Use a variety of media to get the same/consistent message across.
INACCESSIBILITY	Problems connected with physical or psychological remoteness.	Build in 'walking about time' on at least two occasions per week.

it is arguable whether without them it is possible to become an effective manager at all. Figure 6.2 provides an opportunity for you to assess your own communication skills and to identify areas for improvement.

Rate yourself	I believe I have demonstrated these skills adequately ◄———	———► need to improve
Listen actively		
Negotiate		
Say No		
Deal with personal criticism		
Present proposals and sell ideas		
Disagree without being aggressive or rude		
Offer praise		
Criticise constructively		
Contribute to meetings		
Argue logically		
Summarise accurately what others have said		
Avoid interrupting		
Chair meetings		
Redefine problems as opportunities		
Obtain information that people are trying to conceal		
Use questions without sounding inquisitorial		
State complicated things simply		
Handle differences of opinion		

Figure 6.2 Verbal skills required by managers
Source: Adapted from Leigh 1994

Table 6.2 Improving communication in organisations

Controlling the flow of information	in the case study	possible solutions
Need to know principle	Elizabeth confused her audience early on with too much jargon	An A4 sheet with headings about her talk
Queuing	Many of the items could have been held over or communicated in a different format	
Critical timing	By hastily calling the meeting neither was she well prepared nor were her audience ready to receive the bad news	
Prevent isolation from subordinates	Staff felt under pressure	
Off-site meetings	She could have set a better time and more convenient environment	Regular informal meetings with people help maintain contacts
Increase redundancy and repetition		
Multiple channels for the whole message	More time for preparation would have allowed a short briefing paper or headings to be produced	A short telephone call to another centre manager outlining her approach, or better still face-to-face discussion
Redundancy within a message		
Reduce ambiguity in the message		
Use simple and direct language	She used jargon	Informal testing and soundings can often produce valuable feedback
Avoid unnecessary associations		
Use as much face-to-face oral communication as possible	Elizabeth talked instead of allowing people to ask questions	Outlining her 'game plan' for everyone to see would have helped staff focus
Obtain feedback		

Effective listening	Despite her good intentions Elizabeth overlooked the most important component	
Limit your own talking		
Put the talker at ease		When listening train yourself to think – reflect, clarify then speak
Remove distractions		
Be empathic		
Avoid putting listeners on the defensive		Anticipating concern by thanking staff and recognising their input as listeners in the communication process
Go easy on argument and criticism		
Use descriptive, non-valuative language		
Don't club subordinates with your status		
Address objections and arguments to the communication head-on		
Two-sided arguments		
Forewarning		
Repeat main points		
Draw explicit conclusions		
Take extreme position if highly credible		
Make explicit recommendations for action		
Reinforce word with actions		

Source: Adapted from Feldman and Arnold 1985

> **REFLECTION (2)**
>
> *How did you rate your skills as a communicator?*
> *What are your strengths as a communicator?*
> *What are the areas you need to develop?*

If managers overcome the more obvious pitfalls to communication skills they are well on the way to developing communication in the organisation. Improving communication in organisations is conceptualised by Feldman and Arnold (1985) whose work we have used in relation to our case study (Table 6.2).

MEETINGS

It is important that different types of meetings are identified and understood by participants. The convenor has a responsibility to prepare beforehand as well as refining her or his skills as chairperson. Guidelines that would have been helpful to Elizabeth in organising the meeting are shown in Bell's (1988) chart (Table 6.3) which is a succinct outline of the essentials.

> **REFLECTION (3)**
>
> *Which aspects of organisation did Elizabeth founder on?*
> *How could she improve?*

For the participant, the eight questions adapted from the ICI review in Everard and Morris (1990) are still a relevant starting-point for evaluation (see Figure 6.3).

CHECKLIST FOR PARTICIPANTS	VERY	NOT AT ALL
1 Was there a clear purpose to the meeting for all?		
2 Was the attendance correct?		
3 Was everyone sufficiently prepared?		
4 Was time used efficiently?		
5 How high was the commitment of the group?		
6 Was the purpose of the meeting achieved?		
7 What was the quality of the outcome?		
8 Was the action to be taken, and the responsibility for it, clearly indicated with a mechanism in place for follow-up?		

Figure 6.3 Meeting evaluation checklist
Source: Everard and Morris 1990: 52

Table 6.3 Guidelines for organising a meeting

	THE ORGANISATION OF A MEETING
PLAN	Know the objectives of the meeting and what is to be achieved
COMMUNICATE	Inform other team members what is to be discussed at the meeting and why
PREPARE	Prepare room and resources Put agenda in a sequence and allot appropriate time to each item Arrange your papers in agenda order Plan results for each meeting item – know what is to be achieved Decide membership, location, time, duration and notify all those involved Prepare yourself and brief those who are to lead discussion Arrange cover for self and own staff
RAISE POINTS	Declare aims and agenda at outset Work to agenda sequence Put across information clearly and confidently
MANAGE DISCUSSION	Encourage constructive discussion Keep discussion directed toward aims Remain in charge throughout: resist any challenges to your authority Control the pace of the meeting to a time schedule Keep the mood of the meeting good-tempered and objective
CONCLUDE	At the end of each agenda item present sharp, clear conclusions Check understanding and acceptance of conclusions
REPORT	Prepare a report on all important meetings Make report short, concise, listing conclusions against each agenda item If there are agreed follow-up actions, state who does what and when, and who will check
FOLLOW UP	Send out the minutes with decisions and actions to be taken, by whom, by when, listed Check that any agreed actions are successfully carried out

Source: Bell 1988: 191

In preparation for the meeting Elizabeth could have considered the following communications checklist.

Communications checklist

1 Have I taken account of different values, experiences, interests, abilities and habits?
2 Have I tried to express rather than impress in my transfer of communication? Was my message consistent with my past behaviour, credibility and status?

3 Have I chosen the right medium? What use have I made of oral presentations, team briefings, one-to-one talks? Has my written communication been checked for ambiguity and suitability for my audience?

4 Have I tried to obtain the maximum feedback to reinforce understanding, taking account of distraction, distortion and the inevitable simplification by people?

5 Am I aware of the 78 per cent non-verbal element in some messages? How do I attempt to improve my voice, tone style and appearance?

6 Do I maintain my commitment to communication as the essential requirement for effective management?

ACTIVITY

The following six areas provide a useful checklist of influence skills, or persuading behaviours. Elizabeth would have benefited from examining the way she tried to influence others. Use Figure 6.4 to consider Elizabeth's skills/ compare these with your own.

Influence targets	Evidence of achievement	
	Elizabeth	You
1 Ability to have an impact on others by action or through example.		
2 Ability to get others involved in the processes of management.		
3 Persuading staff to balance individual needs and institutional requirements.		
4 Persuading others to consider a wide range of options.		
5 Able to negotiate effectively.		
6 Ability to use a range of strategies to obtain agreement.		

Figure 6.4 Checklist of influence skills

Finally it is worth remembering, 'Even by our silence do we communicate'.

> See yourself as others see you.
> Hear yourself as others hear you.
> Be impacted by your performance the way others are impacted by you.
> (Gilmore and Fraleigh 1993: 85)

Further reading

We begin our selection of further reading with **Managing by Communication** (1982) **Michele and Gail Myers**. This is a comprehensive guide to communication within an organisational setting. The introduction contains the laudable intention of making the book readable, interesting, provocative and current and these objectives are largely fulfilled. Part one begins with a theoretical stance with sections on why we have organisations, what permits people to organise, constructing meanings and developing expectations. The function of communication in organisations and the difference between communication and information are all considered in some detail.

Chapter two considers organisational theories and the implications for communication through a discussion of the classical school of writers (Taylor, Weber, Fayol), followed by the behavioural school of Mayo (the Hawthorne studies) before progressing onto grouping, Likert's four systems of management and McGregor's work under the banner of human resources theories.

Chapter three is devoted to the concept of meaning in information theory, and feedback as it affects organisations, interspersed with some lively examples of the 'bulls-eye' and 'ping-pong' theories of communication (p. 77).

Part two considers the structure of transactions at their various levels in both verbal and non-verbal communication, including spatial and tactile aspects. Confusing and double messages in spoken transactions form a significant chunk of this chapter, which examines categories of message (for example, pre-emptive small talk, informative, evaluative and imperative demands). Message distortion and overload within the context of upward and downward communication structures are discussed together with possible solutions. The chapter on motivation and influence – with Macoby's categories of craftsmen, jungle fighter, gamesman or company man – underlines the diverse influences and motivations that exist between workers, while a section on trusting and developing trusting relationships through risk-taking provides an interesting and varied organisational perspective.

Chapters on leadership and power discuss established theories and are followed by sections concerned with the roles of groups in meetings and decision-making. Managing conflict (chapter 9) provides a further theoretical stance as well as strategies and skills for resolution.

The chapters on presentations and interviewing offer more sound advice through checklists and tables, while a series of exercises linked to each chapter provides further scope for practice and assimilation in a detailed case manual in a complex area.

Improving Your Communication Skills (1990) **Malcolm Peel** is a three-part guide to communication beginning with the initial ingredients, guidelines for success, body language and conventions of conversation.

Each chapter concludes with twenty 'do's and don'ts' that act as a useful summary. The oral presentation chapter contains advice on preparation, analysis, reinforcement, rehearsal and delivery including handling difficult questions. Meetings (chapter 5) begins with a consideration of seating arrangements (p. 91) before tips on effective chairing and recording (see Figure 6.1). The chapter on dealing with the media provides advice on television and radio interviews, relations with journalists, press conferences and launches.

Part two begins with a chapter on written communication and offers suggestions for effective report- and brochure-writing. Here the section on drafting press releases contains some sound advice.

The final part of the book, on communication technology, is somewhat limited given the rapid advances in this area. However, the last chapter on a communications audit provides examples of checklists that could be usefully amended for an early years setting. The overall emphasis is on the practical aspects of communication, with guidelines towards improvement, much of which has relevance within any education setting.

Communication in Schools (1986) **David Trethowan** is one of a series of Industrial Society publications designed to help school managers during a time when business links were very much in their infancy. The first short chapter begins with a case study before moving to an eighteen-point checklist for head teachers. Oral, written and visual communication leads to a section on job descriptions and school handbooks. Chapter 7 provides useful guidance on meetings, although aspects of IT have become somewhat dated. Interpersonal communication is considered under the headings of characteristics of good staff communication: communication facilitators; effective listening and giving feedback.

Similarly, communication with the media addresses the main points of one-to-one meetings with a reporter, using prepared statements and radio and television interviews, the latter containing the warning 'Beware of a telephone call from local radio which may be an interview going out live', as 'words once spoken cannot be retracted'. Evaluating a communication system advocates observation, sampling, surveys and interviews as methods of gathering data and effecting improvements. Designing a communication system is a similar variation on an earlier theme of checking and evaluating. Despite the size of these pamphlets (barely 24 pages), they nevertheless provide some valuable summary data that can be incorporated into most systems or used as a further means towards evaluation.

Chapter 7

Selecting suitable staff

This chapter focuses on: Establishing an effective framework for selection
procedures
Selecting instruments available
Assessment of candidates

In this chapter we examine the ways in which an establishment can set out to review its changing needs and select appropriate staff when opportunities occur for expansion, or replacement of staff. We introduce an expanding school, where Kate, a new head teacher, is able to involve staff in a process of participative decision-making. The process involves seeking out the views of staff, and the outcomes of this consultative approach often lead to greater staff commitment and involvement in the organisation.

We also consider the ways in which the selection of staff relies on the instruments used in outlining specifications for the job and person required and the ways these can be developed, together with issues involved in assessment and decision making.

We find that often a flow diagram (see Figure 7.1) can provide a useful aid for managers and others less familiar with the recruitment process.

CASE STUDY

Kate has been head of Ferndown Nursery and Infant School for less than 2 years and inherited the present staff. The school has grown from a small village infants to a one-form mixed entry nursery and infant school as its location on the edge of town has gradually developed with new, private housing.

However, following a period of low staff turnover and increasing numbers of children on roll, Sylvia, a member of staff, has now retired and Kate has the opportunity to appoint two teachers and one support assistant. The teaching staff who remain in post have a variety of experience and all are keen and willing to consider moves within the school in order to accommodate new staff or for their own professional development.

In preparation for the expansion and replacement of staff, Kate has asked staff to think about their own needs and the needs of the school and to share their views at a staff meeting. It emerges that the staff believe themselves to be well provided for in terms of their individual development, but feel that as a school they are in need of people to develop the curriculum for PE, art and music. They also feel that staff are needed to both maintain and develop partnerships with parents, and to promote liaison between reception and nursery classes as part of an early years unit.

The findings are interesting as the member of staff to be replaced had been responsible for RE, English and Assessment, Recording and Reporting. Thus, it is clear that within the staff there was expertise that had not been used previously, while some people were responsible for areas that they no longer wished to retain. Furthermore, Kate feels that it would be good to encourage applicants from minority ethnic groups because she wishes the school's staff to reflect a wider community than merely that of the local area.

Appointments pages in the quality newspapers show advertisements from recruitment consultants whose job is to guide busy managers towards finding the right candidates for jobs. Clearly schools and nurseries do not enjoy such

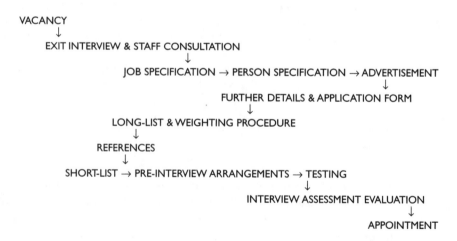

Figure 7.1 Staff selection flow diagram

benefits, which makes it all the more important for their managers to have sound strategies for the selection and recruitment of staff. This is even more significant in the current climate. Research by the Office for Standards in Education (Ofsted) has shown consistently that the main differences between schools and nurseries that are successful and those that are judged to be failing relate to the performance of staff. In this respect, the phrase 'effective recruitment brings both immediate and long-term benefits and is often a determining factor in a manager's success' could not be more appropriate.

Selection of staff, then, is paramount to effective schools and nurseries. It must therefore be seen as a starting-point when heads and governors are given the opportunity to restart the cycle of continuous improvement, replacement or alteration, depending on the circumstances. Consultation and discussion are a vital part of the data-gathering process. In Kate's case she needs to ascertain what kind of replacement is necessary for Sylvia.

Participative decision-making

Kate's first task is to consider the pupil trends within the area. In her case, numbers have risen sharply over the last few years, but she needs to know the longer term predictions. At the same time she can involve governors and staff by obtaining feedback from them as to what they see as future needs. The chart below (Figure 7.2) can be used by a staff group as part of a development exercise.

Any attempt to gather such information depends a great deal on the climate and previous experiences of staff. In the case of Ferndown they had not been used to adopting a more extended professional role so the idea of contribution to the staffing process was unfamiliar. Kate's decision to include everyone was based on her commitment to participative decision-making and stemmed partly from the categories outlined by Owens (1987) in relation to drawing on staff knowledge.

As a staff we are:
Good at
Bad at
Short of
Ready for
Resistant to

Figure 7.2 Feedback form
Source: Day et al. 1985

I   The test of relevance

Teachers and other professionals should participate in areas that concern methods and materials. In a collaborative situation their interest in the person joining the new team should be encouraged as part of their professional development. Kate saw the appointment as part of the development of the whole school. She wanted everyone to think 'improvement'.

2   The test of expertise

Staff experience should be valued particularly with regard to specialist issues or local knowledge, for example certain cultural aspects or parental expectations. All staff had been in post longer than Kate and this was an opportunity to talk through some of the changes she anticipated while respecting their local knowledge.

However it is not just the decision to include staff but their understanding about the level of involvement that is important. These levels of involvement can range from discussion to democratic centralism.

I   Discussion

Clearly there will be certain decisions that staff will feel unable or ill-equipped to participate in. Nonetheless, some limited involvement in discussion, as part of good communications, can only be beneficial and improve morale. This can be shown as

Head teacher's views	Staff input

2   Information seeking

This provides staff with more scope to participate, although the head still retains the majority stake. Not only will she or he have to provide more information, they will also be influenced by feedback. This can be shown as

Head teacher's views	Staff input

3   Democratic centralist

This is perhaps the furthest point for a head, a position where staff views are presented as part of the final process. Although it might appear a high-risk strategy it can lead to increased commitment and motivation. This can be shown as

Head teacher's views	Staff input

Such an approach might appear particularly cumbersome or unwieldy; however the effect on staff, whatever their career stage or level of competence, cannot be underestimated. Trice and Beyer (1984) summarise the arguments regarding staff participation as follows:

1   The process of becoming truly committed to an organisation is accelerated by staff participation in their planning and recruiting.
2   Participation in recruitment stimulates judgements about work itself as well as about candidates and newcomers.
3   Newcomers may prove useful in scanning the work environment and lead current members to discover which new skills and knowledge they should learn.
4   Current members (including those long established) may be alerted to previously unrecognised internal and external demands.

REFLECTION (1)

Consider your experiences of staff participation. How much more could you have contributed to the process?

Exit interviews

These are a means of collecting information from departing employees. One person who knows more about a post than anyone else is the person who is leaving it. Whatever the circumstances – promotion, retirement, a lateral move or even redundancy – there will be experiences that they have gained that can and should provide valuable detail towards formulating the new post. Clearly, the quality and reliability of the information will vary a great deal but the skill of the manager is in being able to dissect those important strands and weave them together with certain new ones into a stronger more effective post.

If the argument for collecting as much data as possible has been accepted, the idea of exit interviews should not come as a surprise. Jeff Grout, managing director of the recruitment agency Robert Hall, refers to them as an important source of feedback about an organisation. A formal, structured and confidential interview, conducted by a line manager or member of the personnel department, will provide the company with useful insights that could be of direct assistance in, for example, recruiting a replacement.

> During an exit interview you can learn how a person's role has evolved. That gives the employer a better idea of what sort of skills and qualifications are required by his successor – or perhaps whether a successor is required at all.
>
> In a recent survey of 150 executives conducted by Robert Hall International, over 40% said that exit interviews provided valuable information

on departmental matters, and more than a third claimed to have learned how aspects of corporate policy could be refined.

(Grout 1995)

Naturally, given the more informal nature of school and pre-school organisations, such an exit interview would appear to be a role for the staff development coordinator as a way of gaining inside knowledge and further reducing possible barriers of status or authority.

Job descriptions

The process of analysing a vacancy needs to be initiated. In the case study the staffing sub-committee had already been briefed about possible options so for Kate what was now needed was a job description. Hilton's (1986) outline provides a useful starting-point alongside the 1995 School Teachers' Pay and Conditions document:

> Job descriptions are a method of supplying sufficient descriptive details of the post on offer to enable the prospective applicant to respond appropriately, by application forms and/or letter. They should be regarded as a stage in the selection process, in that some intending applicants would gather from the CONTEXT and TONE of the job description that they would not wish to proceed further. It is important, therefore, that your detail and working are carefully thought out, in order to convey accurately the desired impression of the school and post.

The following guidelines have been found useful by many primary head teachers:

NURSERY SCHOOL:	Full name needed
POST:	Title and area
SCALE/LEVEL:	
JOB DESCRIPTION:	Place the job within the context of the school, describing its purpose
RESPONSIBILITIES:	TO WHOM the post-holder will be answerable FOR WHOM the post-holder will be responsible WITH WHOM the responsibilities will be shared FOR WHAT the post-holder will be responsible
SPECIFIC DUTIES:	These need to be stated with clarity and directness. The form in which aims are stated is appropriate here: To teach ... To organise ... To develop ... To contribute ...

There could be a final statement under the 'Specific Duties' heading to the effect that the successful candidate may, from time to time, be asked to consider undertaking other duties, but that these would be subject to negotiation.

As Hilton (1986) says, plan the layout of the job specification so that a pattern of information is presented clearly (see the Appendix at the end of chapter 8). Be concise and precise in your statements and choose your words with care, so that you are not misleading about either the school or the post. Whatever outcomes are agreed, every post should contain a 'growth implant' – some aspect of the work that will allow the person to 'learn, develop and in time take on further responsibility'. Drucker (1977) counsels against the 'too small job' but also reminds us of the impossible job, something he terms the 'widow(er) maker'.

REFLECTION (2)

Which posts within your school/nursery provide a space for growth?

Personnel specifications

The job description has described the post and placed it within the context of the school. The next task is to produce a personnel specification that defines the attributes, in terms of qualities, skills and experience, considered to be important in a potential holder of the post.

The following criteria/categories have been shown to be appropriate when considering potential head teachers and could be relevant to other posts.

1   **Career track record** – What work experience is valuable?
2   **Education and training** – What form of initial and subsequent training and qualifications are desirable?
3   **The quality of experience and performance to date** – Define the type of experience that is appropriate and the criteria for judging successful performance.
4   **Motivation** – What indications are given of a strong motivation towards the post in question?
5   **Fitness for this school** – What training, experience and personal qualities contribute to a 'best fit' analysis?
6   **Seal of approval** – What in particular do you like about the information you have so far?
7   **Personality/personal qualities judged from documentary information** – What is the impression gained from the information so far?

Advertisements and further details

Kate was concerned to convey the right tone and style of the school in the details to candidates. As a result, the job was advertised nationally and candidates were provided with an A4 folded information sheet about the school, together with a one-sided job description and person specification.

Kate's decision to opt for a clearer chart format (Figure 7.3) was based on her commitment to involve sub-committee members at all the stages.

A letter to candidates on school notepaper gave the timetable for appointment following the closing date, together with the instruction to bring evidence of recent work in school, designed to consolidate the interview process.

Pre-interview arrangements

Depending on the number of applications, an initial sifting will now be possible based on the person specification criteria. If large numbers are involved, the use of a points scoring system with 3–5 points for essentials (depending on the decision of the sub-committee) and 1 point for desirable should provide sufficient data to create a shortlist of candidates for the next stage. Critics of such a clinical approach believe the essential warmth and personal qualities are discarded in favour of personnel-focused managerialism. This is not the intention, and if it occurs it is due to a lack of clarification regarding the personnel specification together with an under-statement of qualities needed. Hence selectors need to look carefully at job descriptions and specific qualities before proceeding.

Attribute	Essential	Desirable	Assessment
Experience Qualified Teacher	2 years at Key Stage	experience across age range	application form, letter
Education Training	evidence of continuing professional development	leadership role as a coordinator	form, letter, interview
Skills	good orientation and interpersonal skills	innovative approach	pre-interview, reference
Achievements	high standards	whole school project	evidence from candidate

Figure 7.3 Person specification chart

Pre-interview assessment

Given the fallibility of the interview, its limitations and structural defects, it makes sense to consider what alternative forms of assessment exist and are appropriate in the circumstances. These fall broadly into two categories:

1 Supporting evidence from the candidate as to their suitability.
2 Confirmation from a third party (usually written) about the candidate's qualities.

Divided in this way, it can easily be seen which of the two processes has a stronger basis for validity and which one is open to misinterpretation and possible abuse. Clearly very few schools would wish to involve prospective candidates in any form of psychological or psychometric testing. However, recent trials for the National Professional Qualification for Headship (NPQH) contained a psychometric test as part of the assessment profile. Nevertheless, its value to teaching staff in a school or those in a nursery centre setting must remain questionable. Instead the use of group and team building questionnaires has increased. Such interest inventories and value questionnaires should, however, still be treated with caution.

By contrast, references are easy to send, have a high return rate (if accompanied by a stamped addressed envelope) and can often create the illusion of authority and professional judgement. Hence, despite their bland categories the employer can often feel she or he is spreading the blame if the successful candidate does not 'come up to scratch'. Recent legal settlements have awakened selectors to possible pitfalls, and the slow erosion of the 'closed' reference or unseen reference on a candidate is finally being accepted.

One fault is the standardised nature of reference requests, which naturally encourage a standard response. As a result the opportunity to ask searching questions about the candidates' record of achievement, health, attendance and general contribution to a school is invariably lost. The example from Blankshire County Council (Figure 7.4) is typical of many local education authorities. While some head teachers might find time to devise a seven paragraph format, others would seek to circumvent many of the requests and instead submit their own response. As part of the selection process its value is therefore limited.

Because of her fears about receiving a number of bland responses, Kate decided to create her own reference format based on the qualities she felt were important for the post (Figure 7.5). By constructing a specific reference sheet it should be possible to proceed to the interview stage of the process without too much difficulty.

Kate planned to interview candidates throughout a full day, starting at 9 o'clock in the morning. She decided on the following programme. Candidates would be invited at intervals of $1\frac{1}{2}$ hours. Each would be asked to bring a recent

---

Blankshire County Council

CONFIDENTIAL

Dear . . .

Applicant
Post applied for . . .

I should be grateful if you could let me have, in confidence, your views on this applicant's suitability for the above post, details of which are enclosed. These views will enable the Selection Panel to decide which applicants most closely match the agreed selection criteria. Confidential references have been sought on all applicants with the essential educational qualifications and experience shortlisted for interview.

It would be helpful if you would restrict yourself to two sides of A4 paper, using the following paragraph structure:

1   Current and previous contexts for the applicant's work, where relevant;
2   Current range of responsibilities and experience and level of effectiveness in current post;
3   Educational philosophy, professional awareness and preparation for the post;
4   Knowledge and skills, personal and professional qualities;
5   Any relevant additional information;
6   Health and attendance record;
7   A judgement on the applicant's potential and suitability for the post, using as a final recommendation one of the following:

    a)   Recommended, without reservation, for appointment;
    b)   Recommended for appointment;
    c)   Recommended for consideration of appointment;
    d)   Not recommended for appointment;
    e)   Unsuitable for appointment.

The Selection Panel have met and the shortlisted candidates are being called for interview on Friday 15 February. I enclose a stamped addressed envelope and should be grateful for your reply by 14 February.

The Selection Panel have asked me to express their appreciation of your help.

Yours sincerely,

Figure 7.4 Standard reference request

sample of work undertaken as a basis for discussion, together with two photographs of one aspect of their work in school. The deputy head would provide a short tour followed by refreshments, after which candidates would be given 15 minutes to prepare a short talk on one aspect of school organisation decided

Ferndown Infants School

Dear . . .

The following candidate has applied for the post of . . . at our school. At Ferndown we believe in an open reference policy and so the governors and I would be grateful if you would discuss your decisions with the candidate and/or consult widely. Interviews are to be held in the week beginning May . . . so we would be grateful for your reply by the Friday before . . .

I enclose a stamped addressed envelope and thank you in anticipation for your help and support.

Yours sincerely,

Kate Poppythorne.

Name:

Title of post:

Responsibility:

Experience – Please state the groups and classes taught	
Professional Development – In what way has this person developed through new responsibilities	
Suitability – Using the job description, please outline the candidate's particular strengths for this post.	
Working Relationships – What evidence was there of good working relationships with staff, parents and other agencies.	
Health – On how many occasions was s/he absent during the last three years (excluding pregnancy and confinement).	
any other qualities you wish to state.	

Figure 7.5 Specific reference request form

by the panel. Interviews would last no more than 35 minutes with candidates leaving a contact number on departure.

Such arrangements are by no means uncommon and simply reflect the concern a head teacher and governors have for creating a balance between allowing a candidate to demonstrate their skills and maximising the flow of data through the panel.

Interviewing

If these guidelines have been followed within the framework of an agreed selection policy, the final stage, that of a formal interview, should proceed more smoothly with both sides being aware of the rigorous nature of the process.

Selection is designed to eliminate candidates on the grounds of ineligibility. It must not, and indeed cannot, under Equal Opportunities legislation, discriminate against individuals. However, this does not prevent selection panels making decisions based on evidence collected by means of documentation and observation, provided it is matched against the criteria outlined in the personnel specification. The arrangement by which such information is recorded and introduced into the final stage of the process needs to be considered carefully in order to ensure that consistency is maintained. Similarly, the value and weighting of such information in the final decision can only be a matter of professional judgement agreed by the panel **prior to the start of the whole process**.

Such considerations demand a high level of human resource management, both for head teachers and governors. Here local authority and diocesan training courses can provide a valuable resource for training and developing the necessary personnel skills.

This chapter has underlined the need for considerable preparation and structure in the recruitment of staff. As any manager is aware the 'poor performer' or misfit costs much more than the capable or effective staff member. All the more reason to ensure, therefore, not only that the right appointment has been made but also that the post contains a significant element of growth or stretch. As Drucker (1977) reminds us, the number of posts at the bottom is inevitably much larger, so that out of every ten people on a given level no more than two or three can normally expect even one promotion. For teachers it is even more important that posts are designed to provide significance and meaning and not as any pre-determined vehicle for promotion. The need to make the right decisions and maintain performance with a view to development is a major aspect of interviews and interviewing.

Further reading

We suggest the following three texts are worthy of your study. We begin with *Staff Selection in the Primary School* (1990) **Geoff Southworth**. This book identifies a number of areas in need of attention, chiefly unfairness, prejudice, the involvement of lay people and interviewing skills, and then attempts to address these concerns in an opening chapter that appraises the selection process.

The stages of the selection process, the person and the criteria form the bulk of chapter 2, which cautions against pure substitution in vacancies, advocating instead a degree of analysis based on 'patches of responsibility' that reflect the current situation. Guidance on job descriptions and person specifications follow, together with governor's responses to the qualities of a good teacher. Chapter 3 provides a number of case examples from the advertisement stage through to job description and letter of application before concluding with some sample references. These are analysed in subsequent chapters that outline a selection of proforma for initial selection by shortlisting.

Chapter 5 on interviewing contains advice on planning and preparation, questioning and listening and ends with some useful action points. Decision-making and aftercare highlight two of the key elements in the process with clear messages for schools and panels regarding support for both the appointee and those candidates deemed unsuccessful.

Our second text is **Human Resource Management in Schools** (1996) **Roger Seifert**. This recent publication 'seeks to contribute helpful advice to school managers at a time of serious problems as well as some opportunities'. Part one argues for clearer evidence of management as a way of maximising staff performance, and then considers the main elements of industrial relations and the role of the Local Education Authority (LEA). Surveys of head teachers regarding sources of advice on financial delegation, together with guidelines on industrial relations bargaining positions, provide the main ingredients of an informative chapter.

A section on employers and managers includes a survey of relevant employment legislation as well as sections on teacher union structures and beliefs. The final section on custom and practice considers the complexities of extra duties against a background of equity and fair treatment for all staff.

Human resource planning as it affects reductions and redundancy is outlined with examples of model agreements before a chapter on recruitment and selection offers advice on advertising and interviewing from an equitable standpoint. The chapter on pay, performance, structures and grades is necessarily detailed, and leads on to discussions about conditions of service and guidelines regarding the 'management of absence'. Equal Opportunities legislation, together with dissemination, identification and remedies (p. 129), are examined.

The employee relations section begins with tables on disciplining procedures and recommendations as well as case study examples including aspects of grievance and dispute. Communication, consultation and negotiation forms the final chapter that recognises the benefit of consultative committees and collective bargaining in a climate where the introduction of HRM into schools at a time of change and tight budgets has one intention and that is the smooth implementation of lower unit labour costs through cheapening staff costs and intensification of staff work. This may provide accountancy notions of value-for-money, but it will not fulfil the needs of school managers in terms of the chimera of managerial freedom and flexible staff. These can only be met through more traditional industrial relations processes and procedures of negotiating change with and through recognised unions.

(p. 163)

How to Pick People for Jobs (1989) **V. W. Shackleton** is our final recommendation. This is a practical guide for selectors which provides important information on job descriptions and person specifications. The first chapter on recruitment of candidates, including consultants, contains outline questions and guidelines for newspaper advertisements. Selection exercises and case studies provide an opportunity for individuals to review their procedures within a wide range of practical examples.

The chapter on interviewing is similarly valuable with discussions on validity and purpose as well as outline plans and questioning techniques. References and their value precede chapters on testing and its validity as well as the use of supplementary selection methods including in-tray exercises. The principles of selection rather than discrimination make up the final section where check lists and examples guide the uninitiated, before the whole selection process is rehearsed for a model appointment of a secretary that contains this honest conclusion:

No one pretends that assessing people and making selection decisions is easy. It is a truism that people are complex and difficult to fathom, let alone predict what they will do when they work for us . . . One thing is for sure. Nobody ever gets selection right every time . . . what we can all hope to do is to be a little more professional in our approach.

(Shackleton 1989: 212)

Chapter 8

Effective interviewing for selection

This chapter focuses on: Interview preparation
                           Recording and evaluating interview data
                           Decision-making

We examine, in some depth, how those selecting staff should approach the interview procedure, highlighting some of the weaknesses and strengths of the process. We explore ways of recording and evaluating what panels have found out about candidates. We also introduce a panel of interviewers, headed by Sylvia, a nursery manager, who has the task of appointing a number of qualified and unqualified staff to a new nursery.

The case study focuses on the way that staff are recruited. The establishment chosen is striving to work within an equal opportunities framework and the approaches adopted are no different from those in maintained or voluntary sector provision. The case study examines how a private day nursery approaches this most important aspect of effective management. The nursery is in an area of a city near to a large hospital, a number of colleges and a university. The manager hopes to attract families from around the area as well as those who commute to work in, or near, the hospital, and educational establishments. She requires a high calibre of staff for all posts.

CASE STUDY

Bridge End is a purpose-built private day nursery catering for children aged from birth to 5 years old. The proprietor is a growing company with a national reputation for high standards of child care. The company is serious in its commitment to staff and operates an equal opportunities policy. The recently appointed manager and deputy, together with a company representative, have the task of appointing a number of qualified and unqualified staff. All arrangements for the interviews have been organised between the personnel section and the nursery manager, Sylvia, who will act as chairperson throughout the procedure.

Sylvia and the panel have tried to ensure that they will attract a good range of candidates and have advertised the posts in a variety of publications both mainstream and locally based. Information to candidates has been clear and good job descriptions have been prepared. In preparation for the interviews Sylvia has prepared a suitable room with a waiting area that gives access to toilets and coffee facilities. The room has been set out in order to put candidates at ease and low chairs have been arranged in a circle. Sylvia has prepared and shared with the other panel members two sets of questions, one for qualified candidates and one for unqualified candidates. She has allocated groups of questions to each panel member and provided a simple score sheet for recording responses.

Job interviews

No matter how relaxed the surroundings or familiar the people, both interviewees and panels participate in a stressful and, for candidates, competitive situation that can give rise to inconsistent behaviour and flawed judgements. However, despite their limitations, interviews remain an important part of the selection process, as Reed's Personnel Services Survey of 1996 (Figure 8.1) illustrates.

The reasons for people according more importance to interviews are difficult to identify. However, the common myths regarding power, control and lack of preparation remain in the minds of some people. Thus, the definition of an interview as 'a meeting deliberately set up between two (or more) parties for a purpose in the control of one party who asks the questions the other party answers' (Gratus 1988: 6) rings true and highlights the most significant flaws in the process: failure to control the interview and the inability to ask appropriate questions. If these aspects are borne in mind then there is no reason why interviews should not remain an integral component of this important procedure.

It is important to emphasise here that some of these prejudicial factors – namely preparation and authority or status – can come into operation even before the interview stage, and that employers are likely to be influenced by some of these along with the following four areas:

1   **Appearance** – Unkempt appearance and failure to make eye contact were
    seen by the Reed survey as the 'factors most likely to put interviewers off

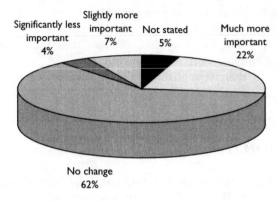

Figure 8.1 Importance of interviews
Source: Personnel Today, 27 August 1996

a candidate'. Clearly there are a number of cultural factors contained in this statement that could give grounds for considerable misinterpretation, particularly amongst members of the ethnic community.

2   **Early decisions** – Many people arrive at a decision regarding suitability within the first 4 minutes of the interview. They then spend the rest of the time seeking 'evidence' to confirm their judgement.

3   **Timing and placement** – Panels take time and need practice to refine their procedures, something that can often militate against the first candidate, or disadvantage the last person who often has to work hard to impress a weary and sometimes disinterested panel. Research suggests a poor candidate can often advantage the next person who shines regardless of her or his superiority (the contrast effect).

4   **Regional variations** – Accents and geography can be another discriminatory factor, depending on circumstance. Such bias extends to research undertaken with the general public regarding credibility and integrity. Variations in pronunciation and departures from the more 'standard English' can often create minor, yet significant, discriminators.

A candidate who is keen to succeed should also remember these points. So, candidates should prepare well before making initial contact with a prospective company or establishment, even before making a telephone call or writing for an application form. In the case study, some of the potential inequalities have been overcome by the commitment of Sylvia and her colleagues to treat employees fairly. This commitment to equality has involved the use of a third party to give information to candidates about posts; a selection procedure using specific criteria for selection and a willingness to understand that not all candidates have access to the same resources such as word processors, which might make a considerable difference to the appearance of one application form over another. This latter point has also been applied in relation to the positive way in which Sylvia and the panel acknowledge that applicants from some minority groups may have English as an additional language, and this is not seen as a barrier to their employment.

Summarising all the research, the key issue remains one of structure and objectivity that demands a conscientious and committed approach throughout the process.

REFLECTION (1)

Compare one interview where you performed well, as opposed to a disastrous experience. What differences in structure and approach did you notice?

Interview arrangements

Translating the need for structure into practical guidelines, Style, Location, Timing, Procedure and Decision-making would appear to provide suitable headings on which to proceed.

Style

The style you choose to adopt underpins the whole process, for at the outset the decision can only be yours as a panel. No matter how informal a candidate may appear, or how casual in approach or answers, you are in control of the process. Conversely, if someone only comes prepared for a set question and answer session, not only will they have not taken the trouble to study the information you have sent, but their degree of participation might well suggest a lack of fitness for the post. Overall there is an expectation that the occasion will largely be formal, one with roles being clearly defined beforehand according to the previous experiences of the panel and nature of the post. The precise composition of the panel is a personal decision within group boundaries, so while two plus members is the minimum, it may be that in appointing a Senior Manager another three to four governors or others may legitimately wish to participate, provided they have been involved in earlier shortlisting decisions. A panel of more than five, just like a shortlist of the same size, often becomes unwieldy and there need to be good grounds for not delegating some responsibilities.

In the case study, three panel members were considered appropriate given the level of the posts, although Sylvia was concerned that such a number might be daunting for unqualified staff. However, the company representative was also able to give vital personnel information and her presence was considered invaluable in the proceedings.

Location

In many schools and centres this can often appear pre-determined. Certainly, if the interview is to be carried out at the workplace, facilities will normally be limited to a head's/manager's room, parents' or medical room, but that need not diminish the impact or its status. However, whatever location is agreed, considerable thought and preparation are necessary so that the maximum information can be elicited from candidates to support the data collected earlier and so help inform the final decision.

Clearly, no layout will suit every candidate and previous experience suggests that even among four to five candidates there can be considerable disagreement over the style of room setting when feedback is sought. However, the use of furniture, particularly tables, is crucial. Just as people can become more upset by the style of message rather than the message itself, so a seating plan designed to allow everyone to have space to write notes behind a table may be perceived as being somewhat intimidating. On the other hand, low chairs designed to reflect informality can often cause problems in joining a group, particularly when the rest are already seated. The general consensus would appear to favour a situation where candidates are asked to join the panel at a table, often close to their guide who has collected them.

Timing

Less than 15 or more than 45 minutes is unusual and suggests a lack of forethought. Once again it is good recruitment practice to agree the same time for all candidates and communicate this before the proceedings in order that they may mentally prepare. However, responsibility for time allocation rests with the chairperson who needs to decide the extent of supplementary questions or variations based on how much time is available during the proceedings. In the case study the time set for qualified candidates was 35 minutes, while unqualified candidates were asked to expect to spend 20–25 minutes in the interview.

Procedure

Planning here is essential, particularly if there is to be no overlap with data collected earlier, and so the WASP acronym (WELCOMING – ACQUIRING – SUPPLYING – PARTING) remains a useful template:

Welcoming

This is the opportunity to set the initial tone of the interview and help put the candidate at ease in a stressful situation. Introductions are never easy, particularly when one's mind is on the content to come. The use of name cards or labels can be of great benefit here, particularly for later in the proceedings when there may be the need to structure and phrase particular answers. Most panels would expect to open with an ice-breaker question that can often help to reassure an interviewee and allow them to hear themselves in a different environment.

Acquiring

The process of asking open-ended questions now begins in earnest. A pre-meeting of the panel should have agreed particular areas, with the chairperson acting as facilitator to ensure as smooth a transition from each area as is possible.

While there is no shortage of guidance for managers and governors, the need to tailor each question to aspects of the job description remains important. The length and content of each answer will determine the extent a panel member feels the need to probe or ask for supplementary information. Such pressure questions are a necessary part of a process that can become increasingly sophisticated, particularly since local authority questions can be matched by technical aspects from sources such as universities on policies or procedures. As a result, panels need to give thought to the use of situational questions that present candidates with a scenario that involves a number of professional decisions, none of which is necessarily wrong. The intention is to focus on what the candidate believes rather than her or his trying to second guess the panel.

In the case study Sylvia was particularly keen to understand the philosophy underpinning each candidate's working practices and so her questions focused upon candidate's belief systems as well as their skills and knowledge. Thus, when it came to a question about working in partnership with parents Sylvia asked candidates to explain how they would respond to an over-anxious parent who made considerable demands on the time of the nursery staff. In their responses, and on the interview schedules, Sylvia was looking for the candidates to be aware of the following:

- sensitivity;
- empathy or understanding of the mother's anxiety;
- ability to listen;
- ability to reassure the mother;
- recognition that if the mother's approach became detrimental to the care and safety of other children the nursery nurse should refer her to the Centre Manager.

Supplying

Leading or loaded questions that give clues about an interviewer's bias are unlikely to provide a true or full answer and indeed might well contravene equal opportunities. Much more important is the opportunity for a candidate to supply any other information or beliefs that she or he thinks will support their application. Such a process can often provide the panel with further insight as to the candidate's suitability and motivation as well as communicating their understanding of the dimensions of the job. Thus a number of minor factual details for clarification might well illustrate excessive anxiety or a lack of preparation.

Parting

The interview needs to be closed decisively, which again is the responsibility of the chairperson. Both candidates and panels need to feel they have given a good account of themselves and that they are clear about follow-up procedures.

Sylvia concluded each interview by reminding candidates that the interview would shortly be terminated and asking them if they had any questions for the panel.

Decision-making

Discussion about candidates is a sensitive issue and often overlooked in the pre-interview arrangements. Whatever system has been employed, it will now be put to its sternest test, for after thousands of words spoken there is only one chance to evaluate each candidate systematically based on written records and matched against the job description.

Anyone with experience of interviewing will be aware of the difficulty of keeping records throughout a candidate's interview, not to mention the endurance needed if all four or five are to receive equal attention. It is for this reason that panels resort to question scoring as a shorthand method of comparing answers. Instead, a more effective way is to provide each panel member with a list of questions and areas one would expect candidates to include, as the following chart (Figure 8.2) illustrates.

If these procedures have been followed, the process of decision-making should be considerably easier. Nevertheless, different interpretations are inevitable and conflicting views occur. However, the purpose of documentation is self evident. The more evidence assembled, the easier it becomes to match candidates against the demands of the post. However, one can never be certain one has made the right appointment and despite the most detailed preparation a high degree of fallibility remains. On occasions this can mean re-advertisement, an increasing occurrence within primary schools at senior level. In no way should this be seen as failure, instead it should be viewed as the rigorous application of a process designed to appoint the best person for the job. Amendments to job descriptions and person specifications can take place after review. However, what is important is that the process has been seen to function effectively.

Having made arrangements to offer the post and secured agreement, the unsuccessful candidates need to be debriefed. Evidence gathered from the interview process is useful in giving full and helpful feedback to unsuccessful

Question	Required responses	Further information Quality of answer
What attracts you to this school?	Challenge Development Personal interest Interest in school Past experience	
How would you develop a whole school policy for assessment?	Consultation Evaluation of consultation Documentation Implementation Evaluation of scheme	
What kinds of assessment are available and which do you think is most appropriate for children entering school from a nursery?	Summative Evaluative Formative Informative Other information (expansion)	

What problems would you foresee for a newly qualified teacher?	Realistic expectations
	Proper reporting – of a
	   factual nature
	Know the next step –
	   natural progression
	Enhanced performance
	Match tasks to child	

What are your strengths as a professional?	Extra curricular Experience Volunteer Personal interest Enthusiasm	

How would you handle a complaint from a worried parent about 'testing'?	Initial response
	Support from the person in
	   charge of assessment
	Discussion with head
	Recording of events with a
	   view to handing over to head	

Figure 8.2 Required responses to questions

candidates. In the case study, Sylvia encouraged unsuccessful candidates to contact her for feedback so that the information gathered through the interview could be of use to them in future job applications.

This chapter has focused on one of the most important aspects of human resource management, the interview process. The opportunity for professionals to engage in discussion with others outside who have a legitimate interest should not be dismissed, as it remains an integral part of the accountability process for everyone working in the public sector.

Further reading

We suggest you try to obtain local authority guidelines on recruitment and selection as a basis for improving your own practice. Some general examples can be found in the Appendix that follows.

APPENDIX

This appendix sets out examples of recruitment and selection policy and procedures, as well as providing a suggested set of materials that may be used during the process.

Recruitment and selection policy

The council will recruit and select all employees in an equitable, effective and efficient manner that will ensure the provision of the appropriate personnel able to meet service requirements.

These guidelines set out the practices and procedures that must be followed in order to enable the council's policy to be achieved. They are directed at all those who are involved in the recruitment and selection process at whatever stage. It is essential that these guidelines are fully understood and observed in 'word and spirit'; training is available.

Adherence to the guidelines will ensure that:

- recruitment decisions are made in a fair and equitable manner based on objective criteria;
- the most suitable person for the job is appointed and, therefore, high standards of service are maintained;
- applicants are not discriminated against;
- the council can demonstrate that it is a good and credible employer that deserves the confidence of the public;
- allegations of unfair treatment can be successfully resisted.

There is a commitment to keep the policy and the guidelines under review – changes will be made to reflect developments in good practice and the law or if the guidelines are found to be in need of refinement in the light of operating experience.

Equal Opportunities in recruitment and selection

The council is committed to providing equality of opportunity to job applicants and those who use council services.

The council's Equal Opportunities policy states: '. . . no job applicant must receive less favourable treatment on the grounds of age, disability, sex, sexuality, marital status, race, religion, colour, nationality or requirements which cannot be shown to be justifiable.'

It is important that those who are involved in the recruitment and selection process have an understanding of the law relating to Equal Opportunities and the potential for discrimination if a systematic and objective approach is not applied. It is the duty of every employee to avoid and eliminate discrimination.

Discrimination can arise in a number of ways, some of which are not necessarily obvious. It is important to appreciate the distinction between direct and indirect discrimination:

Direct discrimination

This is treating a person unfavourably because of their race or gender, while disregarding their ability to do the job, for example, not appointing a woman because she is married.

Indirect discrimination

This occurs when a requirement or condition is applied, which, whether intentionally or not, adversely affects women, men or a particular racial group considerably more than others and cannot be justified. For example, insisting without good reason on a maximum age of 28, as women are less likely than men to be available for work below that age because of child bearing.

The following provides a summary of the current law relating to discrimination:

The Sex Discrimination Act 1975 and **Race Relations Act 1976** state that it is unlawful to discriminate against a person in employment because of their race, gender or marital status.

The Disabled Persons' Employment Acts 1944 and **1958** encouraged employers to look positively at the employment of disabled people. Some provisions of the above legislation have been repealed by the **Disability Discrimination Act 1995** which has employment provisions that will come into force at the end of 1996 to make discrimination against disabled people because of disability unlawful. A disabled person will experience discrimination if incorrect assumptions are made during the recruitment and selection process about how the person's impairment may affect job performance.

A particular impairment may have no effect whatsoever on the ability to do a job or it may be made irrelevant by the provision of specialist equipment or by adaptations to the workplace. The fact that the workplace may be inaccessible to a disabled person does not justify exclusion from the shortlist or discrimination when an appointment is made. Grants are available from the Placement Assessment and Counselling Teams of the Department of Education and Employment for equipment required by a disabled person in order to carry out the duties of the post, and also for physical adaptations to the workplace.

Further guidance on the above Acts can be sought from the council's Access Officer or Equal Opportunities Policy Officer within the Chief Executive's Department.

The Trade Union and Labour Relations (Consolidation) Act 1992 made the refusal of employment on grounds related to a person's union membership or non-membership unlawful. This includes situations where the person refused employment does not satisfy the requirements of a job advertisement concerning union membership, or where a practice exists whereby a union approves members for employment. Refusal of employment would include measures such as causing the person to withdraw her or his application, or offering the position on unacceptable terms.

The Rehabilitation of Offenders Act 1974 states that certain convictions become 'spent' after a specified period of time. Those with spent convictions are not required to disclose the conviction on application forms if asked to do so, as any failure to disclose a 'spent' conviction is not a lawful reason for dismissing or excluding a person from employment.

Exclusions from the above legislation

Race or gender as a Genuine Occupational Qualification (GOQ)

Discrimination on the grounds of race or gender in the recruitment process is unlawful except in certain specific circumstances. These circumstances are governed by Section 5(2)(d) of the Race Relations Act and Section 8(2)(e) of the Sex Discrimination Act. These allow employers to restrict applications for employment to one race or gender where the job involves providing persons of that racial group or gender with personal services promoting their welfare and those services can most effectively be provided by a person of the same racial group or gender. It is advisable to quote the relevant sections in advertisements for such posts – where this is felt to be necessary, the Personnel Division must be consulted before including any statement to this effect in a job advertisement.

Exceptions to the provisions on 'spent' convictions

There are certain exceptions to the provision on 'spent' convictions which are relevant to local government employment. These are set out in the Rehabilitation of Offenders Act 1974 (Exceptions) Order 1975 (SI 1975 No 10230), as amended by the Rehabilitation of Offenders Act 1974 (Exceptions) (Amendment) Orders 1986 (SI 1986 No 1249 and SI 1986 No 2268). Typical examples include any employment concerned with the provision to persons aged under 18 of accommodation, care, leisure, social services, and so on.

All job descriptions for posts that are exempt from the Act must include a statement to this effect under the Special Conditions heading. Advice must be sought from the Personnel Division on what areas of occupation the above legislation covers.

Monitoring

Effective monitoring of recruitment and selection is essential to ensure that the council's Equal Opportunities policy and discrimination legislation is being adhered to. Monitoring also enables the Authority to meet the requirements of Equal Opportunities performance indicators and is recommended by the Equal Opportunities Commission and the Commission for Racial Equality in Codes of Practice which may be taken into consideration at an industrial tribunal.

To enable recruitment monitoring to be undertaken, monitoring forms are issued to all applicants for vacancies within the Authority. Statistics are compiled in departments to monitor the stages of the recruitment process, provide reports to appropriate committees and inform future recruitment decisions.

Recruitment and selection procedures

Examples of procedures to be used during the recruitment and selection process follow.

Information to prospective applicants

Minimum information pack

The level of a post will influence the amount of information to be sent to applicants. Literature sent to prospective applicants for senior officer posts will differ from that sent to applicants for, say, clerical positions. The question that should be asked is what does an applicant need to know and what additional information should reasonably be provided to enable her/him to come to a view on whether or not she/he would wish to work for the Authority. Cost will be a consideration. In all cases, it is good practice to send applicants relevant supporting information with the application form.

The following information should be sent to all applicants as a minimum:

- Job description and person specification (see Figure A.1).
- Application form with guidance notes.
- Equal Opportunities monitoring form.
- Conditions of employment.
- Where and to whom application forms should be returned.
- Reminder of closing date.
- Details of any selection tests and assessment methods.

As a matter of good practice, departments may also wish to consider enclosing details on:

- Selection process including dates of interview etc.
- Aid to recruitment scheme (where applicable).
- Police checks where substantial access to children will be involved.
- The Rehabilitation of Offenders Act 1974.

EDUCATION DEPARTMENT JOB DESCRIPTION

Job Title: Nursery Nurse   **Location:** An educational establishment
                                         Division: Infant/Nursery/Special Schools

Grade: Scp6–15

Responsible to: Head teacher or another designated teacher
Responsible for: Not applicable

Job purpose: The care and welfare of specified children within the education establishment and to assist in the education process

Main Duties:

1   Providing limited involvement with the curriculum.
2   Joining in with the activities of the children in classes.
3   Supervising children, usually in the presence of a teacher.
4   Acting as a point of contact with parents.
5   Providing general care and welfare services for the children.
6   Maintaining a safe environment.

Organisation Chart

Head teacher

|

Deputy head teacher

|

Class teacher

|

Nursery nurse

Qualifications and Experience:

Essential: Certificate of the National Nursery Examination Board or equivalent
Desirable: Previous experience in an educational establishment
Special Conditions (if applicable):   None
General: This job description is a representative document. Other reasonably similar duties may be allocated from time to time commensurate with the general character of the post and its grading.

All staff are responsible for the implementation of the Health & Safety Policy so far as it affects them, colleagues and others who may be affected by their work. The post holder is also expected to monitor the effectiveness of the health and safety arrangements and systems to ensure that appropriate improvements are made where necessary.

The Authority has approved a policy on Equal Opportunities in Employment and copies are freely available to all employees.

Figure A.1 An example of a job description

Prospective candidates should not be invited to contact a nominated person for an 'informal discussion'. This is bad practice and can contravene Equal Opportunities legislation.

Application form

All applicants must complete the Authority's standard application form which is accompanied by guidance notes. CVs alone must not be accepted.

Preparing for the interview/selection tests

Informing the candidates

1   Give candidates at least seven working days notice of the interview/selection tests.
2   Write to all candidates informing them of:

   - date, time and venue of interview (enclose map of location and access details, if appropriate);
   - any selection methods which are to be used in addition to the interview;
   - names and post titles of the selection panel;
   - estimate of how long the interview, selection tests, etc. will take;
   - dates reserved for any further stages of the process if necessary (for example, second interview);
   - the need for qualification certificates and other documents (such as a driving licence) relevant to the job to be presented at interview;
   - a person to contact if they have any particular requirements like wheelchair access or a communicator.

3   Encourage and welcome school leavers to bring along their National Record of Achievement.
4   Unless candidates have expressed a wish for their referees not to be contacted prior to interview, write to referees.

Selection panel preparation

The panel must each have a copy of the job description, person specification and interview assessment sheets. Preparation for the interview is essential, and the panel must meet in advance and allow sufficient time to plan the structure, conduct and content of the interview, agreeing questions and reminding themselves of the rating method to be used.

Conducting the selection interview

All members of the panel must be free from other commitments during the interview period. All the panel members must be involved in each interview.

In the interests of equity, all candidates must be asked to respond to the same range of pre-determined questions that relate to the criteria on the person specification. These questions will, however, need to be followed up by additional relevant questions which will probe or clarify a response or statement made by a candidate to enable the panel to thoroughly assess each candidate's suitability.

Questions based on assumptions regarding personal circumstance must not be asked. If it is considered necessary to assess whether personal circumstances will affect performance (for example, jobs involving unsocial hours or requiring mobility) questions should be objective, related to job requirements and the applicant's ability to meet those requirements. Such questions must be asked of all applicants.

Attendance records should be discussed with all applicants at the interview stage.

When the panel has concluded its questioning, the candidate should be given the opportunity to ask questions and/or make a short statement in support of her/his application.

Following the conclusion of each interview, individual members of the panel must each assess the candidate using the council's candidate assessment form (see Figures A.2 and A.3).

Once individual assessments have been recorded the panel will discuss their individual ratings with the objective of reaching an overall consensus on the final ratings to be awarded to each candidate. These must then be recorded separately using the consensus interview assessment form (see Figure A.4).

Where a presentation has been part of the assessment, panel members will need to share their assessments of this at this stage. These will have been recorded on the council's consensus presentation assessment form (see Figure A.5).

The findings from all selection methods used, including the interview, should be considered collectively and then, based on all the evidence, the panel should reach their final decision.

In order to confirm the panel's final decision, references should now be consulted.

Candidates should be ranked in an order relative to the outcome of the interview/selection tests. Should the successful candidate decline the offer of appointment, the panel may wish to offer the post to the next candidate in the rank order.

All records of the interview process must be retained on file for **twelve months**.

CANDIDATE ASSESSMENT FORM – EXPLANATORY NOTES

1 Attribute

The experience, skills, knowledge, etc., that have been identified on the person specification for assessment at the interview stage must be identified under this heading.

An indication of whether each attribute is essential or desirable (as shown on the person specification) must be given.

2 Assessment

This is an indication of the extent to which the candidate satisfies each attribute in the opinion of the interviewer.

The interviewing panel should agree a recording scheme **before** the interviews take place. The following is suggested:

A   Candidate fully satisfies the specified attribute
B   Candidate possesses the attribute but not to the extent specified
C   Candidate does not satisfy/possess attribute
D   Unable to assess from information sought/provided

3 Comments

A brief note should be made to support each assessment particularly where B, C or D are awarded.

4 Overall assessment

Each interviewer should make a brief note under this heading of her/his overall assessment of the candidate in terms of whether or not the candidate has demonstrated from the interview the ability to do the job.

5 Consensus view

At the conclusion of the interview process, the panel should determine which, if any, of the candidates is the best person for the job by evaluating the outcome of the interviews together with the assessment exercises that may have been undertaken.

Candidates who do not satisfy all the essential attributes identified on the person specification **must** be rejected.

Figure A.2 Candidate assessment form notes

CANDIDATE ASSESSMENT FORM   **CANDIDATE:** _____

Attribute	Assessment	Comments

OVERALL ASSESSMENT:

_____

_____

_____

Figure A.3 Candidate assessment form

CONSENSUS INTERVIEW ASSESSMENT FORM

Post: _____   Dept: _____

Candidate: _____

Date/Time of Interview: _____

Attribute	Assessment	Comments

Figure A.4 Consensus interview assessment form

CONSENSUS PRESENTATION ASSESSMENT FORM

Post: _____   Dept: _____

Candidate: _____   Date: _____

Topic: _____

Assessment: A = Fully satisfies the specified criteria
              B = Possesses the attribute but not to the extent specified
              C = Does not satisfy/possess attribute
              D = Unable to assess from information sought/provided

NB: The panel must agree the purpose of the presentation before seeing any candidates.
    The attributes to be assessed should be listed below.

Attribute	Assessment	Comments

COMMENTS:

_____

_____

Figure A.5 Consensus presentation assessment form

After the interview

Offer of appointment

The selected candidate should be offered the post verbally as soon after the decision as possible. The offer must then be confirmed in writing. All offers of appointment must be made subject to satisfactory references, confirmation of qualifications, medical clearance, probation and police check (as appropriate). The candidate must be advised not to give notice to terminate their current job until confirmation of these has been given.

Commencement

As soon as the above conditions have been met, a start date should be agreed with the successful candidate. Written confirmation of this including the date, time and place of reporting and name of the person who will meet the successful candidate should be sent. Ideally, as a matter of good practice, some indication should be given of how the first day/week will be spent including induction arrangements.

Contract of Employment

A written statement of particulars must be issued to a new recruit within two months of the start date. A proforma Statement of Terms and Conditions of Employment can be produced.

Unsuccessful candidates

It is good practice to notify candidates that they have been unsuccessful as soon as possible and to offer them constructive feedback.

Induction

The line manager/supervisor will be responsible for ensuring that an appropriate induction programme is organised for each new recruit.

Probationary period – monitoring progress

New entrants to local government service are required to complete a six month probationary period. Regular meetings between the manager/supervisor and the new recruit during the induction period are essential in order to enable the individual's performance to be monitored and for her/him to raise any queries or concerns or seek assistance in adapting to her/his new employment. As a minimum, review meetings should be held once every four weeks.

At the end of the probationary period, the new recruit should be informed of whether or not she/he has been successful. This should be confirmed in writing.

Reviewing the process

A candidate accepting a job offer does not automatically signify that the recruitment and selection process has been a success. It is good practice to examine every recruitment exercise with a view to assessing whether anything could have been done better. Following from this, it may be possible to identify training needs or changes that need to be made to current practices. Any suggestions for improvements to the guidelines will be welcome.

Complaints

Any candidate who has reason to believe that she/he has been treated unfairly or discriminated against at any stage of the recruitment and selection process will be requested to submit their complaint, in writing, to the Assistant Chief Executive.

The Assistant Chief Executive will seek comments from the department concerned and ensure that the complainant receives a single response on behalf of the Authority.

Chapter 9

Adding to the value of the workforce

This chapter focuses on:	The role of management in staff development
	Understanding and assessing individual needs
	Coaching and cooperative techniques designed to promote commitment

> What must change is the way we manage the only unlimited resource we have – the value adding – capacity of the workforce.
>
> (Gilmore and Fraleigh 1993: 75)

Although the above quotation is a general one and not directed specifically at schools or nurseries, it still has enormous relevance for all those responsible for human resource management (HRM) in educational settings. Such reluctance can often be traced to questions about the value of 'off the job' activities that upset established routines unnecessarily. Underlying all this is an implicit questioning about enhancing a person's prospects for the benefit of another employer. Furthermore, when resources are stretched and pressures increase, the temptation to restrict activities to general policy statements and statutory appraisal interviews becomes even more attractive. Equally, the demands of external inspection have tended to encourage teachers to perform well on a familiar stage rather than embark on any risk taking that might be subject to adverse comment or poor gradings. The same may be true of the professionals in full day care or private and voluntary sector provision. Clearly, the balance between effective performance and professional development is a sensitive one, where any initial dip in competence as a result of conversion or redirection needs to be carefully monitored and supported.

CASE STUDY

Mike, Acting Head of Millbrook Junior, was displaced in the amalgamation of Millbrook with Millvale Infants and Nursery to form a new primary school, Brookvale, on the infant and nursery site. As part of his new role, Mike will be responsible for the transfer of staff and children to the new site from the old junior building as well as staff development coordinator. Recent long-term absences by experienced staff, and temporary cover by newly qualified teachers has placed considerable pressures on ancilliary and support staff as well as highlighting the need for a thorough review of staff development activities.

REFLECTION (1)

How should Mike begin to develop a programme for the new Brookvale Primary School?

Mike began with the following aims which he discussed with the new head teacher.

The newly amalgamated school should develop a culture of professional activity where

1   Each individual is valued and respected.
2   Ownership of a programme is encouraged through a mission statement leading to discussions on priorities that are understood by all.
3   Evaluation of activities occur through staff review, short-term monitoring and longer interviews that record developmental needs.

In formulating these proposals, Mike first took account of the following quotation made over twenty years ago but still valid today.

What is needed is a dynamic model of professional development in which the responsibility of every employer, every head of school or *nursery* (our italics) or head of department, is to ensure that the teachers for whom they are responsible are performing at the very highest level of their capability. Not all teachers are, or ever will be, the best teachers anyone could wish, but all teachers should be given the tools and training to enable them to become the best teachers that they individually can be. To have such teachers is, at the very least, the right of every child.

(*Trends*: DES Magazine 1977)

Second, Mike provided staff with the following policy statement as a starting-point.

> It is recognised that the ethos of the school depends very much on the welfare of the staff. It is therefore necessary that job satisfaction is felt by all with positive benefits to the school community. A meaningful staff development programme is therefore essential.
>
> Staff will be encouraged to plan their own personal development in consultation with the head teacher and colleagues. Needs will be identified – both strengths and weaknesses will be met by in-house and extra mural INSET.
>
> External agencies will be sought as appropriate. Staff will be encouraged to share and develop skills and interests both within and beyond the school.
>
> Opportunities for new areas of responsibility will be made available.

Third, Mike asked every staff member to consider:

- the curriculum areas in which they felt most confident and to indicate their degree of strength on the chart shown in Figure 9.1;
- the management areas where they had exercised responsibility and to indicate their degree of strength on the chart shown in Figure 9.2;
- other aspects of staff development from Figure 9.3 and to indicate their priorities along the continuum.

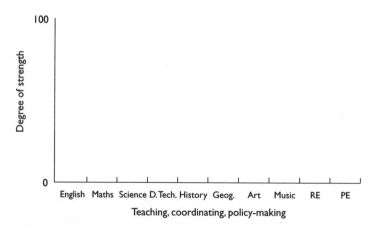

Figure 9.1 Confidence in curriculum areas

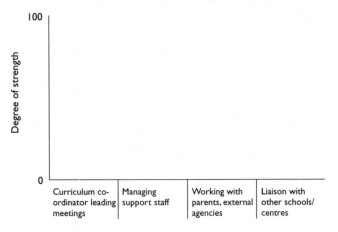

Figure 9.2 Management areas of responsibility

	Not very useful	Of considerable value to me

1   Professional development/discussion of needs

2   Working alongside others – apprenticeship/mentor/job shadowing

3   Mutual lesson observation

4   Exchange of teachers

5   Cooperative teaching, planning, evaluating

6   School-based courses/in-service days

7   LEA/out-county courses

8   Cluster activities

9   Staff meetings as INSET

10   Membership of working parties/committees

11   Staff conference

12   Visits to other schools, nurseries or centres

13   Study groups/seminars – changing membership

14   Guided or self-guided study and research

15   Membership of professional/learned bodies

16   Use of staff library/resources

17   Use of curriculum centred library/resources

18   College of HE/university dept of education library/resources

19   Management meetings

20   Individually designed programme of self study

Figure 9.3 Aspects of staff development

Results were coordinated to determine any particular patterns and to help identify individual needs and aspirations within a broad framework. The intention was to balance the school's needs, as outlined in their development plan, with staff aspirations and expectations.

Career stages

Mike was aware that staff views on continuing professional development would be influenced by previous experiences and current status. Hands (1981) outlines these categories as:

1   those who are frustrated in their ambitions;
2   those who are happy to be in their terminal posts;
3   those likely to gain (further) promotion.

However, this would appear too simplistic given the enormous changes in education and takes little account of individual circumstances that can also be subject to alteration. It might be more appropriate, therefore, to see staff aspirations in a diagramatic form that underlines the need for development opportunities (Figure 9.4). Such a model highlights the dynamic nature of staff development along with the integral role played by the school or centre.

Whatever decisions are made and regardless of aptitude, there remain certain professional needs that can be identified. Morant's four main types (Figure 9.5) have been amended slightly but still remain relevant.

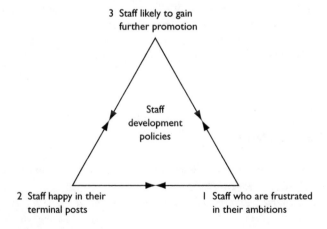

Figure 9.4 Staff aspirations triangle

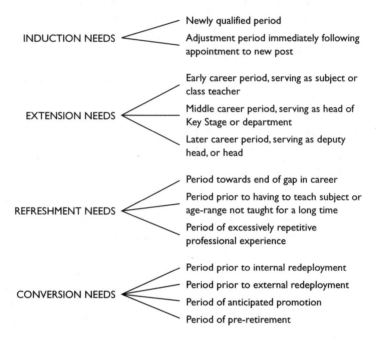

Figure 9.5 Morant's four main types of professional needs

Coaching

Another approach to staff development is for experienced teachers to work alongside those newly appointed, both to help and note areas for development. In recent years many schools have adopted a mentoring programme that broadly encompasses many of these ideas. We see coaching as focused and short-term, during which time the coach identifies specific opportunities and areas to increase competence. The following plan (Figure 9.6), amended from Francis and Woodcock (1982), is a starting-point for managers.

REFLECTION (2)

Consider two areas from your early work where you would have benefited from some coaching.
As an experienced teacher which two areas could you offer as a coach?

Name/job title: ....
1 *Opportunities:* What tasks could be given as coaching assignments?
2 *Choice:* Which new areas of competence does the person need to develop?
3 *Targets:* What realistically can be achieved?
4 *Timing:* How long will this take to achieve?
5 *Tactics:* How will you brief and prepare the person for the assignment?
6 *Monitoring:* How will progress be monitored?

Figure 9.6 Coaching plan designed for senior staff
Source: Francis and Woodcock 1982

Monitoring and recording staff development

Just as important as developing a staff development policy and programme is the need to remind staff about its ownership. While schools and centres have yet to go as far as the 'new employment contract' referred to by Rosabeth Moss Kanter (1990) in *The Change Masters*, their expectations of staff are moving rapidly in this direction.

> Hereinafter the employee will assume full responsibility for his own career – for keeping his qualifications up to date, for getting himself moved to the next position at the right time, for salting away funds for retirement, and, most daunting of all, for achieving job satisfaction. The company, while making no promises, will endeavour to provide a conducive environment, economic exigencies permitting.
>
> (Kanter 1990)

REFLECTION (3)

How do you currently record development activities?
One approach is shown in Figure 9.7.

ACTIVITY

1 What are the key criteria by which you evaluate your work? List these in the left hand column in Figure 9.8.

Personal Evaluation Form

Other Professional Activities

I The Activity (Brief outline)	**2 The Time** (devoted to the activity)

3   The Nature of Personal Involvement (Organiser/Participant)

4   Personal Evaluation (This will include a statement of (a) the value of the activity to the professional development, and (b) a reflection on the management skills exercised and those required)

5   Endorsement (Observations of a critical friend)

Signed .... Date ....

Figure 9.7 Personal evaluation form

2   How do you know when you are successful in your work? What are the indicators or 'flags' that help you to know when you are doing a good job?

Note: You are permitted to use abstractions in the 'criteria' column (for example, 'good discipline', 'providing educational leadership'), but your 'indicators' should be concrete, specific and observable signs of your chosen criteria. You will probably need to identify more than one indicator for each criterion.

Criteria	Indicators of success
1	
2	
3	
4	
5	
6	
7	

Figure 9.8 Role perceptions analysis
Source: Kemp 1981

Audit yourself	Reasons
1 Have I, in the most recent period of my career, maintained a steady upward progression in my responsibilities, authority and rewards?	
2 What were my personal ambitions for this period, and did I achieve them?	
3 Do I have new ambitions for the next period, and do I know what plans the organisation has for me? Do I see any conflict there? If so, how can I resolve that conflict? Is it insoluble?	
4 What new skills have I acquired recently? What opportunities was I given (or could I create) to practise my existing skills?	
5 How confident am I of my chances of progress within this organisation?	
6 How well do I get on with my colleagues? With my superiors?	
7 How well do I think I fit into my school/centre?	

Figure 9.9 Self-audit
Source: Adapted from Hoare 1987

Self-evaluation

This has always been an integral part of professional activities, whether formally or informally. Two differing approaches are to be found in Figures 9.7 and 9.8.

Further evidence of this need for self-examination can be found in the idea of the Sigmoid Curve and its links to career planning. Handy (1994) talks about us 'starting slowly', 'experimentally and falteringly, we wax and then we wane' like an S-shaped curve.

The secret of constant growth is to start a new Sigmoid Curve before the first one peters out. The correct place to start that second curve is at point A, where there is the time, as well as the resources and the energy, to get the new curve through its initial explorations and flounderings before the first curve begins to dip downwards.

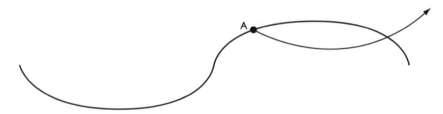

That would seem obvious were it not for the fact that at point A all the messages coming through to the individual or the institution are that everything is going fine, that it would be folly to change where the current recipes are working so well. All that we know of change, be it personal change or change in organisations, tells us that the real energy for change only comes when you are looking disaster in the face, at point B on the first curve.

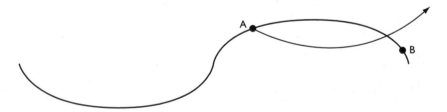

The message for individuals is clear: develop how you wish to before someone develops you.

Giving and receiving advice

ACTIVITY

Your 27-year-old coordinator has recently been promoted to a deputy headship of a large nursery. She has no formal management qualifications and feels that her previous experience has been narrow.

Although you do not have sufficient information to make a detailed assessment, rank the items in the order that you believe would be the most useful developmental experiences for this person. For example, if the individual can have only one of the experiences, which would you advise? Rank this number one and so on.

1   Course in school finance and policy-making (1 day)
2   Counselling session with head (8 hours)
3   Study visit to other schools (3 days)
4   Course in interpersonal skills (2 days)
5   Time off to read Education Management textbooks (2 days)
6   Participation in team-building sessions (2 days)
7   Consultant help on use of time (1 day)
8   Management of stress (2 days)
9   Seminar – The Sociology of Large Organisations (2 days)
10 Assignment Project – The Management Role of the Deputy (4 days)
11 Temporary assignment – Mentoring in various schools (1 week)
12 Training in leadership theory (2 days)
13 Regular meetings with other new deputies to discuss common problems (4 half days)

(Adapted from Francis and Woodcock 1982)

In the original version of the above Activity the authors sought solutions from senior managers in commerce and industry who, not surprisingly, were unable to provide an agreed list. Our experience of working with head teachers and senior staff over a decade has been similar. Nevertheless, the headings have probably stimulated more discussion than any other aspect of professional development. Despite any clear ranking certain areas have been identified as having most value. The opportunity to undertake study visits to schools, linked to counselling sessions with the head is clearly a major priority.

Training in leadership theory and participation in team-building sessions have often also been identified as valuable. Courses in school finance and policy-making are thought to be important later in post, while the opportunity to attend regular meetings with deputies should be part of regular networking opportunities. Time management is an important tool (see chapter 1) which should allow the creation of a slot for textbook reading. As a new postholder it should be hoped that stress management would be a lower priority – unless one attended too many seminars on 9 (The Sociology of Large Organisations)!

In conclusion, what is needed is a commitment from all managers in the service that staff development is a priority for everyone. The following checklists (Figures 9.10 and 9.11) provide a useful summary of some of the key issues for any manager to consider with other senior personnel responsible for staff development.

Throughout this chapter we have chosen to concentrate on the individual and school approaches to staff development. We have ignored staff appraisal, which is a statutory requirement to be undertaken by all maintained schools.

	In place for some time	Just started	Planned but not yet in place	Not yet considered
1 Effective recruitment procedures				
2 Induction course to school for all staff				
3 Appointment of tutor or mentor				
4 Aims and objectives for school and/or nursery				
5 Agreed job descriptions				
6 Up-to-date staff records				
7 Opportunities for all staff to study and discuss changes in policies and procedures				
8 Opportunities to update subject matter and skills, in working time or out				
9 Support for all staff with weaknesses or difficulties				
10 Opportunities for staff to observe others teach				
11 Working parties internally or externally				
12 Help with career prospects, applications, interviews				
13 Annual interview				
14 Opportunities for job rotation				
15 An effective appraisal system				

Figure 9.10 A staff development checklist for the head and Staff Development coordinator

Personal   **Has the newly appointed staff member:**

- Been allocated a work and storage space?
- Been given remission for class contact for support and staff development sessions if she/he is in their first year?
- Been informed of opportunities for in-service training and staff development?
- Been referred to one particular colleague who will act as a mentor and guide during the first year at the school?
- Been given an opportunity to participate in school events (extra curricular activities, committees, etc.)?

Timetable and   **Has the newly appointed staff member been given:**
responsibilities

- A personal timetable of teaching?
- Details of rooms?
- Information about the level and content of the courses on which she/he is to teach/contribute?
- Introductions to outside agencies and others that she/he may come into contact with?

The department   **Has the newly appointed staff member been given an overall picture of:**

- The nursery or school, its aims, development and plans?
- Her/his specific responsibilities within the area?
- The services provided by the centre for other schools or units?
- The liaison between the department and the LEA support service?
- The year plan of meetings (internal and external)?

Administrative   **Does the newly appointed staff member know the**
procedures   **procedures for:**

- Registration?
- Pupil non-attendance and lateness?
- Staff sickness and absence?
- Absence cover for colleagues?
- Other formal school and LEA procedures (e.g. expense claims)?

Resources   **Has the newly appointed staff member had explained:**

- School policy on resource and financial management?
- What resources and materials are available?
- How to order books and materials?
- How to get materials produced: reprographic, photocopying, type facilities?

Figure 9.11 A checklist for those responsible for new staff
Source: Adapted from O'Sullivan *et al.* 1988

However, it should remain an additional and necessary requirement of effective school management.

Finally, rather than provide further reading, we have chosen to include an induction and mentoring programme researched by three head teachers in the North West as part of their Postgraduate Certificate award in Education Management.

An induction and mentoring programme

In a sense the interview itself could be regarded as the beginning of that often neglected process – the induction programme.

(Day, *et al*. 1990)

1   The day of the interview

- Introductions
- General arrangements for the future visits
- Contact names and telephone numbers

2   Before the post is taken up

- Documentation   *only simple and essential*
  for example, staff handbook with day-to-day procedure, topics and schemes of work. If possible there ought to be someone to discuss these with.
- Visits   *head*

  To discuss any arrangements, e.g. mentor.

  mentor or contact

  To discuss documentation and planning.

  departing teacher

  For information on the children, classroom organisation and record keeping.

  core subject coordinators

  To discuss schemes of work.

  children

  Those to be taught by the incoming teacher to make them familiar.

Those currently in the age group to get an awareness of expectations.

- Pastoral   *accommodation etc.*
  May be more likely to help a newly qualified teacher (NQT) than an experienced teacher as there may be less life experience and less choice in the move.

3   First term

An experienced teacher needs to know the procedures and systems and be able to go to someone for advice and help, possibly requires a named contact. An NQT requires more structured mentoring procedures.

- Meetings   *mentor*

  Weekly meetings to discuss:
  Planning
  Assessment
  Classroom organisation
  Strategies
  Discipline
  Children causing concern
  It is important to discuss issues raised by the NQT, not just the mentor.

  coordinators

  To discuss subject issues.

  head

  One per month or half term with mentor if possible. Progress reports or discussion of difficulties which are beyond the scope of the mentor.

- Observations   *of the new teacher*

  By mentor once per half term.
  By head once per term.

- Non-contact
  time courses   To prepare, review and evaluate NQT courses run by county.

4   Rest of first year

- Meetings   Frequency will depend on the quality and confidence of the teacher. Support should still remain in place but a stepping down of the level may be appropriate.

- Observations   Continue as appropriate.
- Non-contact   Continue.
  time
- Courses   Continue.
- Parents   Support in terms of advice before, possibly during to
  meetings   help with difficult questions, particularly in group
                   meetings.
- Review   Both the teacher's progress and the effectiveness of the
                   mentoring system should be reviewed at the end of the
                   first year.

5   The second year

- Continuation?   The teacher should be able to manage with a low level
                   of support.
                   Based on need but must realise that they can go for sup-
                   port whenever they need it – it is not a sign of weakness
                   or failure – we all need it.

Chapter 10

Caring for customers

This chapter focuses on: Identifying customers' needs

Projecting a positive image

Maintaining customer satisfaction

with examples of how you can market your school or nursery, develop the 'image' you want and keep your customers satisfied.

We begin this chapter by illustrating how nurseries and schools have had to change their approach to marketing, and introduce Mrs McKay, the proprietor of a private day nursery, who is concerned about why her business is not progressing in the way she and her business partners had planned. Although it is set in this context we emphasise that this chapter is not simply for those who see themselves in the private sector – it is also instructive for those in the voluntary and maintained sectors as well.

The concept of customer care is one which has been slow to take off in non-commercial enterprises such as nurseries and schools, mainly because in the past such establishments presented themselves on a 'take it or leave it' basis. In other words there was little concern to 'sell' the establishment since such establishments usually 'sold' themselves. However, increasingly schools and nurseries are entering a much more competitive arena, where two significant influences have led to them having to change their approach. The first of these is that there has been an emphasis on the need to work in collaboration with parents as partners in their child's education, while the second is that of greater competition for children between one establishment and another. The result is that the idea of 'the customer' has established itself firmly, and that nurseries, schools and playgroups have to be aware of the image they present to the public, the effect that image has upon their place in the 'market' and the way that this image can be shown to best advantage.

Many might find this a depressing thought, but it is none-the-less a reality, and one which should not be dismissed without considerable discussion and honest reflection by all those presenting themselves as carers or educators of young children. Psychologists have shown that people make judgements about others within the first two minutes of an interaction and then spend the remaining time in looking for evidence to support the view (see chapter 8 on interviewing). This is a sobering thought and should alert anybody wishing to impress others to the importance of 'first impressions'.

So, customer care may seem out of place in schools and nurseries but, whether we like it or not, it is here to stay. In the case study we invite you to consider how Mrs McKay and her staff present themselves and their newly opened nursery to the public; the amount of information they communicate about themselves and their beliefs without even speaking, and the factors that contribute to the development of a positive public image.

REFLECTION (1)

Can you recall being either impressed or 'put off' by your first impression of a school or nursery? How quickly did the impression form? How much information did you need to reach your decision?

CASE STUDY

The Hollies Private Day Nursery

An old house set in its own beautiful grounds on the edge of the London commuter belt, 'The Hollies' is a newly converted nursery which currently caters for twelve babies and twenty-four two year olds. It has opened to meet increasing demands for high quality, flexible provision, and serves mainly professional parents and their children. The proprietor and her staff are strongly committed to providing appropriate care and education for children and expanding to capacity as laid down by the local authority Registration Team.

The building has been well preserved to maintain its original character, yet at the same time it appears light, airy and safe. The gardens have been carefully planned to maximise their benefit to young children. They provide a large grassy, wild garden, a challenging adventure area with climbing frames and safety surfaces, and two safer areas for the younger ones.

Staffing is strictly within legal ratios which allow for 50 per cent of staff to be qualified and 50 per cent to be unqualified. Affordable housing within easy

Table 10.1 Nursery staff

Staffing role	Name	Qualifications
Proprietor	Mrs McKay	BSc
Manager	Eleanor	B.Ed. (Hons)
Deputy	Bharti	NNEB, ADCE
	6 Nursery Officers	all NNEB
	6 assistants	unqualified

reach of The Hollies is in short supply and as a result the staff group are quite unusual in that the qualified staff are mainly younger women with transport or lifts available, while the unqualified staff are local women who have brought up their own children.

Senior management

The manager of the nursery is a qualified teacher who trained to teach primary aged children of 7 to 11 years, and has had no early years experience. Her main subject at college was science, and she is very keen to emphasise this aspect of education. She is well supported by Bharti, who is a very able nursery nurse with several years' experience, although she has previously only worked in one other nursery.

Staff group

All the other NNEBs are either newly qualified, or have had only one year's experience. The remaining staff, some of whom work on a flexible part-time basis, have all had some experiences of working with children in a paid or unpaid capacity, mainly within their families. One has been a playgroup helper. Two others have helped in schools with reading. One taught pupils in a secondary school before her own children were born.

The issue

It is taking time for the team to 'gel', although there is no open ill-feeling between staff. However, Mrs McKay realises that things are not right when her business plan target, relating to numbers of children, is not met. She considers whether she should let some staff go or whether something is wrong with her marketing plan. She decides to discuss the problem with her staff and realises that she must bring about change as quickly as possible. After a discussion between Mrs McKay and her staff, the decision is made to 'buy in' the services of a consultant to help them meet their targets, review their marketing strategy and get their practices, policies and procedures right.

The solution

The consultant's work begins before she ever visits the nursery. Her initial analysis of the nursery's image is that staff sound rushed and rude when they answer the phone to her. She deduces that while all staff are very aware of the importance of making a good impression on prospective parents, they are not so aware that their reputation relies on the way they relate to all members of the public. She notes this in her observations. Next, she requests a brochure from the nursery and examines it looking for 'hidden' messages that tell her about the ethos of the nursery and the values and beliefs it espouses. Finally, she is ready to visit, and she combines this with spending a few minutes in the local area to search for relevant clues.

During her visit to the nursery the consultant identifies a number of things which alert her to potential difficulties in meeting targets and marketing the nursery and she attributes much of this to communication – the way staff respond to one another and to other people.

Points raised by the consultant in her feedback

1   Staff seemed aware that it was important to be very pleasant to prospective parents but some staff were dismissive of others, particularly people like the domestics and cleaning staff.

REFLECTION (2)

What does this suggest about how children in such an establishment might be treated?

---

2   Next she wondered if staff were aware that the public would judge the nursery by the standards, attitudes and behaviour of any one of them whether they were working at the nursery or shopping in their own time on the high street.

REFLECTION (3)

What issues does this raise in terms of confidentiality, loyalty and personal philosophy?

3   She noted that there was emphasis in the documentation on the educa-
    tional experiences of older children while little was said about the
    educational aspects of caring for the younger children.

REFLECTION (4)

How do care and education relate to one another?

---

4   After talking to parents she discovered that staff were inconsistent in the
    ways they communicated with parents, and some staff made some of
    the younger mothers feel intimidated.

REFLECTION (5)

How do we train staff to communicate with others?

---

5   Finally, she concluded that the staff and the proprietor were working very
    hard at some things, while leaving others to chance.

REFLECTION (6)

*How much time do you put aside to reflect upon your priorities –
as a manager, or within your staff group?*

Examining 'image' critically

A good starting-point for any establishment in developing its image is to
engage the services of a 'critical friend', such as a consultant whose task is to
give honest feedback about the organisation's 'public face'. Such feedback is
necessary if an organisation is to improve its image and gain credibility in the
marketplace. Another useful strategy is to adopt a self-evaluative approach,
where members of the staff group reflect upon the image of the organisation.
Try the exercise (Figure 10.1) and compare the answers of staff.

If gaps exist between people's perceptions and reality in relation to your
setting, and they surely do, a way to counteract this is to focus upon how to
market the establishment in order to achieve success and bring closer together the needs of all parties. One way of reducing this gap is described as
developing a 'client-orientated philosophy' and could be helpful in improving

ACTIVITY

Imagine that you are going out to do some market research about the image of your service.

1   Write down the four key words that you think people might say about your service

_____   _____

_____   _____

2   Now write down the four key words that you would *like* people to use

_____   _____

_____   _____

Figure 10.1 Self-evaluation form regarding image

A more daring exercise is to conduct an Image Perception Profile (Figure 10.2), first by staff and then by parents or carers whose children attend your establishment.

Put a cross over the dot which best describes the impression you have about the nursery or centre in each of the following areas:

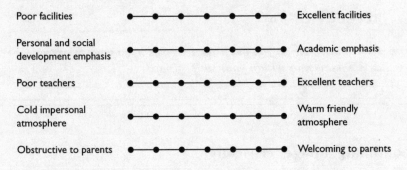

Figure 10.2 An Image Perception Profile

REFLECTION (7)

How close are the views of your staff in relation to the image of your nursery or school?

Issues for the establishment	Focus for discussion with the whole staff	Examples of the ways of progress
The importance of the client	Establish who the clients are Quality of contact in person, writing or by telephone is the key to a successful relationship Clients do not interrupt our work; they are our work	Staff in-service to identify: Who the clients are Establish that the clients come first and that they learn about the nursery or school through the way we communicate
Responding to clients	The attitude with which staff tackle problems and look for positive solutions is most important	Clients expect their problems to be solved and expect to be treated seriously, courteously and sympathetically
Never letting the client down	Keeping promises made either verbally or in writing is fundamental to keeping the right approach as is developing the clients' collective beliefs in the effectiveness of the service you provide	How do we communicate to clients that we value them and will try never to let them down? When we do convince them of this we will demonstrate that our service is client-led
One impression of the school or nursery or many?	All staff should be aware that every exchange with clients may be critical in the 'chain of events' which form a client's opinion of the institution	Remembering that this is 'the all-important encounter', no matter how apparently inconsequential, is a good point to begin at if we are to develop positive impressions
Ensuring that the school or nursery provides a service as well as a product	The balance between providing a product and offering a service is a fine one, which when tipped can lead to client dissatisfaction	There is more to what we are doing than we think. It is important to remember that if we feed and change a child we are providing a service but that service will be increased or lessened relative to the way we approach the child, its carer and the situation
Managing a high-quality service approach	Many issues surround this but the key to success is in defining standards and ways of dealing with clients – this will demand time both for staff training and discussion	Ask what would it be like if I were a stranger in this establishment and it was my child here, what would I want? Would I find it here – all the time?
Developing a new philosophy	It may be useful to remember that all the buildings, organisational structures and staff exist only to provide the client with quality education and care	So how can we work in partnership with our clients in order to achieve the best for all our children?

Figure 10.3 Developing a client-orientated philosophy
Source: Adapted from Davies and Ellison 1991

an establishment's image (Davies and Ellison 1991). The process focuses on seven elements that contribute to achieving a comfortable public profile for a school, but we believe that the same process will hold good for any early child-hood setting. Figure 10.3 has been adapted from this work and illustrates how organisations can, through self-evaluation, see themselves from the outside and change the public's perceptions of them.

It follows from the approach suggested that there are a number of 'stake-holders' in any organisation and these will be similar whatever establishment we are in. A model is illustrated in Table 10.2. The stakeholder illustration can be shown as a 'wall' that is bonded by the different layers, and can be used in staff-development sessions to illustrate the importance of each 'brick' to the whole establishment. If each 'stakeholder' is given equal space in the 'wall', that is, status in the organisation, it becomes clear that the contributions of each staff member are equally powerful and should not be underestimated nor undervalued.

Table 10.2 Stakeholders – bricks in the wall

Proprietor Head teacher Nursery manager	Caretaker	Administrative staff
Parents Carers	Deputy manager Deputy head teacher Shareholders	Nursery nurse
Teacher	Children	Cook
Domestic staff	Support staff	Peripatetic staff

Improving the image

The tasks for the proprietor of The Hollies Private Day Nursery must be to review the way her staff have developed their philosophy, what training needs exist in the light of the feedback received and how she and her staff have pre-sented themselves to the public for appraisal. Next is the need to consider how, using the feedback from the consultant, she can set about changing the pub-lic's perception of the nursery in order to attract new clients and retain estab-lished clients. This has been described as developing 'public relations practice' which is: 'The planned and sustained effort to establish and maintain goodwill and mutual understanding (*within and*) between an organisation and its pub-lic' (Institute of Public Relations in Greenhall 1987: 14) (our italics).

According to this discussion three key elements apply to organisations such as schools and nurseries when developing public relations. These are that they must:

- be **planned** – not a series of ad hoc actions or reactions;

- be based on **mutual understanding**, in other words getting to know the public you are serving, rather than attacking them with publicity, is recommended;
- **take account of the various types of public**, identified earlier as 'stakeholders' and comprising parents, children, teachers, nursery officers, ancillary helpers, governors, management committees, employers, welfare agencies, the local community and other schools, nurseries or establishments with whom such groups might have a relationship such as pre-school groups or toddler groups.

Devising a sound public-relations policy

Devising a sound public-relations policy will inevitably take time since its success relies on the need for 'ownership' by all those who develop it. Mrs McKay, the proprietor of The Hollies, should begin by reasserting first principles and beliefs about the kind of place the nursery endeavours to be. She could use the 'stakeholder' matrix approach to show that every staff member is just as important as the next one, illustrating that without the support and commitment of any member of staff the organisation is weakened. A good indication of acceptable ways of treating others is to ask individuals how *they* would wish to be treated. Reference to the points raised by the consultant shows that 'some staff were dismissive of others, particularly people with low-status jobs, such as domestic and cleaning staff'. Mrs McKay may need to explore her own attitude in relation to this, just as any proprietor, manager or head teacher who, in trying to get on with the main job, may overlook the importance of the contribution made by all staff. Clearly, as the second reflection point highlighted earlier, if staff treat one another in unhelpful ways this suggests that children and others may at some time be treated in the same way. It is important to remember that attitudes are fundamental and it is upon these that establishments such as schools and nurseries may stand or fall.

Further work with staff may reveal a lack of understanding of their ambassadorial role in the local and wider community. Visible identity such as logos and badges can both provide rich sources of publicity and be the impetus for negative evaluation. In her work for The Hollies, the consultant could not ignore the impact the nursery had on the local community and her discovery that one member of staff was critical of some of the things that went on there. This was displayed for all the world to see in the logo on her distinctive turquoise sweatshirt. She had made no secret of her feelings about the way that the staff 'ignored children when they were behaving "badly"'. Clearly, this member of staff was not certain about behaviour policy and about why staff at The Hollies promoted positive behaviour with praise and endeavoured to reduce unacceptable behaviour by ignoring it, where appropriate. Another reflection point suggests that confidentiality, loyalty and personal philosophy are important, particularly when recruiting staff as well as when training needs are identified.

qualities to consider when recruiting staff

A further area for establishments to consider is a frequent review of their documentation. In the case of The Hollies, it is evident that some staff have either failed to understand the significance of their work with young children, or they have failed to communicate effectively to parents the type of work that they do with younger children. If the first were the case, Mrs McKay has a significant amount of work to do in educating her staff and perhaps herself about the experiences of the younger children. These are emphasised in documentation in terms of 'care' rather than in relation to other aspects of children's development, which inevitably must involve cognitive and language development as well as physical, emotional and social aspects of development. This reflection point was raised earlier.

To reduce inconsistency in approaching parents, the staff may need to consider through in-service training what it is like for parents to receive messages about themselves or their child, and how best to share their assessments of children with parents and carers. This approach could considerably reduce the 'intimidation of some of the younger mothers' identified in the consultant's report.

Finally, it is important for The Hollies, and indeed all organisations, not to waste their efforts and hard work by leaving some things to chance. The value of training is worth a great deal more than the initial investment and is necessary if all staff in an organisation are to develop professionally. Similarly, it is important to invest time in creating the desired 'culture' so that staff have opportunities to question, discuss, review and develop their understandings of the procedures, policies and philosophy of the establishment. Failing to create a shared philosophy is surely a major stumbling block for any group whose beliefs are the standard by which they will be judged.

Attracting and retaining clients

One approach to this area is to begin either with aims and philosophy (the centre) and work outwards, or to begin at the outside, that is with the image and the impact of your establishment, and work inwards back to aims and philosophy. In the case study much of the 'heart' of the organisation, that is beliefs and aims, are well established, while the 'peripherals' which are on the outside are less well defined. Wherever the starting-point it is important that at some stage in the developmental cycle organisations should audit themselves very closely in order to identify those areas at which they are successful, as well as to locate those where there is still work to be done. Figure 10.4 is an example of an adaptation of such an audit that links to key words in Figure 10.1 and the perception profile in Figure 10.2.

A significant number of questions need to be answered to ensure that The Hollies improves its image and expands its provision. Some of the issues managers should consider and plan to examine with staff follow.

Buildings and grounds	Hollies response	Action
Do the buildings appear attractive? Are the play areas well maintained? Is play equipment safe, appropriate and challenging?	Excellent appearance commended in the local press and by conservationists Yes, checked daily a.m. and p.m. Yes, checked daily as above and commended by Registration Team	Maintain present quality
Location		
Is the nursery easy to reach? Is there appropriate parking for clients? Do we provide adequate support for families who are unable to bring their children?	Accessible by motorists, lacks frequent bus service Yes No	Review No action required Consider developing a collection service for some clients
The 'caring' nursery		
Are we seen as a caring nursery by staff, parents and children? Do we always go out of our way to find solutions to problems? Are we approachable to parents and others we meet in the course of our work? What indications are there that we welcome people in our nursery? How do we support parents? How do we seek feedback about the service we offer?	Not by all staff Most parents seem satisfied with us Children are very happy here	Communicating our behaviour policy so that all staff under- stand it and feel confident about it Ensuring all parents are satisfied with our approach to caring Maintain this at all times
Records		
What is the purpose of our records? Who contributes to records? How do we approach record-keeping? How do we achieve consistency in maintaining records? How do we share what we know about children and parents? How do we support parents in recording their children's progress?		
Quality of children's experiences		
Is our planning based on individual children's development? Is our planning informed by our observations of children? Is our planning developmentally appropriate? Is our planning focused on first-hand experience and opportunities for talk? Do children have opportunities for choice? Do children have helpful routines based on their needs? Do we share our plans with parents, students and others? Are the experiences we plan purposeful? Do we provide some regular, recognisable experiences as well as some novel experiences? Do we use both the indoor and outdoor environments?		

Figure 10.4 Organisational audit
Source: Adapted from Dennison 1989

How can we improve our public image?

Answering these questions should lead to a discussion of how staff communicate about the nursery and may help The Hollies staff to think about their contribution to its 'public image'.

Who is appraising us?

Who are our customers?

What tells them about us?

What do we want them to think about us?

How can we achieve an image that we want?

How do people complain/tell us they are pleased with us?

What is our mission statement and how can we judge we are meeting the objectives within it?

How do we know what our customers want?

How do we respond to their requests?

How can we improve our communication skills?

How do we address people with whom we work?

How do we address people outside the nursery?

How does our literature communicate our philosophy and aims?

Is the literature we produce clear, accurate, well presented? e.g. the brochures; children's paintings, pictures, etc.

How do we communicate between ourselves?

How do we communicate an unwanted message? e.g. your son bit another child today or your child had a fall in the play area

How do we cater for equal opportunities?

What do we mean by equal opportunities?

What messages are presented in the environment in the choice of resources; books; pictures; photographs?

What messages do we give about choice of food – this could be related to catering for special dietary/cultural preferences versus traditional meat and two veg.

What messages do staff give out in the way they relate to parents, children, one another?

Further reading

We have chosen two titles for discussion in relation to caring for customers, each one designed to reflect the diversity of this subject. Customer care requires regular review and evaluation. Before one employs an external consultant much valuable work can be achieved by adopting a consulting perspective of your own. Later an informal network of practitioners can be established.

Management Consulting Skills (1988) **Charles Margerson** is a handbook used by many independent professional advisers who are seeking to improve their practice and skills with sections on effective versus ineffective styles, strengths and weaknesses and putting knowledge into action. The first chapter provides an outline of the complexity of the process where the twelve main consulting steps are discussed. This leads to the key processes of contracting and time structuring including informal consultations.

Interpersonal skills focusing on solution-centred and problem-centred situations provides another valuable chapter, before questions of access and permission are considered in some detail. Establishing one's own consulting model contains the useful analogy of the:

- consultant as doctor – curing illness or disease in organisations
- detective – based on the principle that something is wrong and there is a need to find the person or persons responsible
- sales person – selling a product or service will be the appropriate solution
- travel agent – seeing the client embarking on a journey and discussing various routes

(Margerson 1988: 103)

These roles provide a valuable reflection point for any professional, coming as they do before the chapter on how managers in similar situations can help each other with the consultancy issues.

The final section on politics and pressure looks at power influences, how to identify sources of influence, gain support and handle negative responses based on an understanding of people's roles and their 'scripts in the change management' process. Keys to success and failure in assignments provides a succinct conclusion to a valuable text.

Some keys to success and failure in consulting assignments

Failure can be caused by:

1 Not involving influential persons early enough.
2 Proposing solutions before problems are diagnosed.
3 Presenting reports full of content without an equal regard for the process of discussion.
4 Moving too quickly, causing surprise and creating defensive behaviour amongst clients.
5 Not recognizing the effect of change in one part of the system on another part of the system.

Success is usually dependent upon:

1 Spending time in understanding the cues and clues.
2 Accurate summaries of issues raised and effective conversational control.
3 In-depth contracting and agreement to ensure an action is on a solid base.

4   Attention to the political processes of the client's organization and the involvement of the relevant people.
5   Delivery on time to the required standard.
6   The management of the assignment by establishing a structure through which all involved can resolve issues.

(Margerson 1988: 185)

Strategic Marketing for Educational Institutions (1985) **Philip Kotler and Karen Fox** is one of the acknowledged source texts for anyone interested in marketing in an educational context. Part one considers the benefits of marketing and discusses the concerns that some people may express. This is followed by the core concepts of needs, wants and demands, along with the components of a marketing environment. Image definitions and their measurement are followed by a chapter on gaining information and identifying marketing problems.

Part two begins with the planning process including steps in design and formation of a marketing plan. The importance of the environment, its opportunities and threats are all reviewed against a case-study background of marketing strategies for American state universities, including the well-known Boston Consulting Group (BCG) matrix of:

- stars – successful programmes in high-quality fields;
- cash cows – programmes in low growth fields that nevertheless command a high share of the market and so produce revenue to underwrite other areas;
- question marks – programmes in high growth fields where the organisation has a low market share;
- dogs – programmes that have a small market share in a declining field.

Market measurement and forecasting is another important section, and contains the following questions:

1   *Who is the market?* Defining who is 'in the market' assists in determining market size and in designing and promoting programs for them.
2   *How large is the current market?* Measuring the current market demand for a program or service helps the institution set realistic expectations for enrolment or participation.
3   *What is the likely future size of the market?* Market forecasting permits the institution to plan ahead. For example, if market demand is likely to drop, a school may prepare to cut back staff or may strive to develop programs that will attract more students. If demand is growing, the institution can plan a response.

(Kotler and Fox 1985: 159)

The chapter on understanding consensus and choice process contains much that is relevant to school and pre-school settings, as does the following chapter on the core benefits of education. The authors examine how these core benefits need to be packaged and augmented with other features to underline commitment and value. The chapter on price and its relationship to quality is important for a consumer and provider perspective, and particularly relevant for private nurseries. Chapters on communicating with the public and collecting feedback, and choosing the right media in the public-relations process as part of establishing the right image are valuable sources of information and guidance. The final chapters on attracting and retaining students can be modified to provide valuable feedback and checklists in an increasingly competitive environment.

Chapter 11

Managing conflict and stress

This chapter focuses on: Causes of conflict
Approaches to conflict management
Understanding and management of stress in the
workplace

We begin by focusing on how conflict arises and ways of handling conflict, before exploring the factors which cause stress. The case study illustrates factors which lead staff in a family nursery to become confrontational when they consider their jobs and expertise to be threatened. We then examine the ways in which managers can handle conflict, before considering stress and its effects on workers.

Conflict in the workplace is not a new phenomena. What has changed, however, is the scale and dimension of the problem leading to a much greater acknowledgement of the issue by managers at all levels, together with a search for understanding and resolution. There are many definitions and interpretations of conflict with the common denominators being disagreement and opposition between people. Owens (1987) is one of the few education management writers to distinguish between conflict and hostility. Malevolent hostility can lead to 'nefarious attacks'; 'These are characterised by (a) the focus on persons rather than on issues (b) the use of hateful language (c) dogmatic statements rather than questions (d) the maintenance of fixed views regardless of new information or argument and (e) the use of emotional terms' (p. 246).

The key difference between such attacks and legitimate expressions of conflict lies in the motivation behind them, often not easily discernible. Given the pressures schools and centres face, it is no surprise that such behaviour is on the increase. Lippitt (1983) reports a survey of over 250 American executives who revealed that they saw conflict as a topic of growing importance and one that already occupied a quarter of their working time. As a result they placed conflict management alongside communication and decision-making as one of the key attributes and important management competencies. Clearly education is no different, and given the enormous changes in legislation, conditions of service and demands from external agencies, all to be achieved with limited resources, the resulting opposition is inevitable. However, since that conflict exists throughout all modern organisations the challenge to turn a threat into an opportunity through skilled managerial action becomes even more important. Traditionally any antagonistic behaviour was seen as avoidable and caused by trouble makers. Luthans (1985) refers to *'boat rockers'* and *'prima donnas'* (our italics) who refuse to go through the right channels or wait their turn, and see the accompanying scapegoating by management as being inevitable. Current thinking contradicts this view and sees conflict as an integral aspect of change management. This, when handled properly, can result in better ideas and approaches, clarification of individual views and renewed interest and creativity, often regarding long-standing problems that would otherwise remain beneath the surface. Diagnosing and remedying the situation depends not just on individual interpretation but also on the ensuing action and decision-making to prevent some people feeling defeated and demeaned, and others mistrustful and suspicious, with a resistance to team work, all of which can increase staff turnover and lower morale.

CASE STUDY

Primrose Street Family Centre is an old one-storey 1940s building which, though brightly decorated, has had little structural alteration, leaving it very basic in design and rather unattractive from outside. The staff are used to the building and become increasingly concerned when, without consultation, a new centre is developed only a short distance away. When they learn that their own building is to be run down over a period while the new centre establishes itself as an innovative community centre containing many facilities, the staff become concerned about job security, when the new building will be completed and who will be expected to remain or move during the period of transition.

The health visitor attached to the local clinic discusses rumours she has heard with Marilyn, a nursery officer at Primrose Street, telling her that she has heard 'on the grapevine' that the newly appointed manager will want only 'younger staff with new ideas'. Marilyn considers herself to be in a good position for future employment at the new centre since she has recently completed a degree in Early Childhood Studies at the local university. She is fairly discreet about what the health visitor has told her, but later in the week when she is irritated by Jean, an older colleague, she remarks, within Jean's hearing, that being experienced at a job does not necessarily make somebody better at it. She then adds that 'some people' will be surprised about who gets the jobs at the new centre.

Issues

Both Marilyn and Jean regard themselves as more competent than the other, and they see themselves in competition rather than collaboration with one another. Jean is threatened by the differences between the skills and knowledge new nursery nurses bring to the job compared with her own. This is summed up by her own training which she says focused on 'damp-dusting and hygiene' compared with 'attachment theories and cognitive development' which is all younger nursery nurses seem to know about, in her view. Marilyn does not find it easy working alongside Jean and others, whom she views as 'blinkered and old-fashioned, yet experienced and powerful because of their knowledge of families in the local community'.

The result of these differences, together with the added anxiety of the new building, create tensions that affect their working practices considerably, leading to the involvement of the manager, Wanda. In supervision with each individual she discovers what has led to the hostility between them, and reflects later upon ways of handling the conflict.

The solution

The management of conflict requires both careful diagnosis and the selection of a resolution style best suited to both parties. Thomas (1977) outlined a model (Figure 11.1) which has become an accepted benchmark for managers. Figure 11.2 provides further explanation of the process.

An examination of the principal causes of conflict together with Figures 11.1 and 11.2 might lead the manager, Wanda, to seek a solution which will achieve harmony and allow each nursery officer to feel they have not been degraded or defeated. Using Figure 11.2 should lead Wanda to decide that:

- quick decisive action is vital;
- she must merge insights from people with different perspectives and help Marilyn and Jean work through the feelings that have interfered with their relationship;
- the issues may be tangential or symptomatic of other issues;
- both members of staff could be helped to learn from their mistakes.

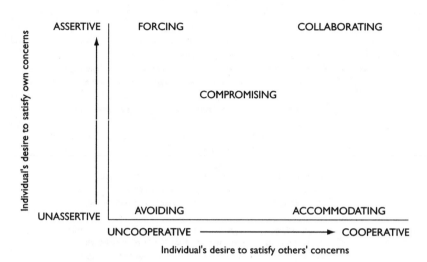

Figure 11.1 A model of conflict handling styles
Source: Adapted from Thomas 1976

The principal causes of conflict

Communication in its various forms often lies at the heart of many disagreements. Misunderstandings, inappropriate language, both in tone and style, excessive talking and inadequate listening together with a lack of openness can combine to make the spoken word or gesture a fermenting cocktail of frustrations that often explode into irritable interaction and dispute. The way jobs are structured, including procedures, rules and resources is another area of dispute, where limited resources and the inevitable budget cuts intensify feelings and exacerbate frustration. Specialist staff and competing departments, often with limited career opportunities, can create a breeding ground for frustration and tension. Here also a person's perceptions of unjust treatment will affect work motivation as well as driving them towards conflicting behaviour as a basis for restoring their status or self esteem. This might include possessiveness about a particular work environment or territory that they have captured either formally or through custom and practice over the years.

Regardless of the cause, the question of personality remains a major factor in the equation. So, while communication inadequacies may be the same for all staff within a school or centre, it may well be that only certain workers view this as an issue. Likewise each person's 'tolerance rating' is different, causing disturbances or minor protests among some people where others would readily explode. Clearly, personality traits, previous experience, age and background all play a part in the internal control process.

Often the key to managing conflict successfully is to be aware of its source

Conflict Handling Styles		Appropriate Situations
Competition	1	When quick, decisive action is vital.
	2	On important issues when unpopular actions need implementing.
	3	On issues vital to the organisation's welfare and when you know you're right.
	4	Against people who take advantage of non-competitive behaviour.
Collaboration	1	To find an integrative solution when both sets of concerns are too important to be compromised.
	2	When your objective is to learn.
	3	To merge insights from people with different perspectives.
	4	To gain commitment by incorporating concerns into a consensus.
	5	To work through feelings that have interfered with a relationship.
Avoidance	1	When an issue is trivial, or more important issues are pressing.
	2	When you perceive no chance of satisfying your concerns.
	3	When potential disruption outweighs the benefits of resolution.
	4	To let people cool down and regain perspective.
	5	When gathering information supersedes immediate decision.
	6	When others can resolve the conflict more effectively.
	7	When issues seem tangential or symptomatic of other issues.
Accommodation	1	When you find you are wrong – to allow a better position to be heard, to learn and to show your reasonableness.
	2	When issues are more important to others than yourself – to satisfy others and maintain cooperation.
	3	To build social credits for later issues.
	4	To minimise loss when you are outmatched and losing.
	5	When harmony and stability are especially important.
	6	To allow subordinates to develop by learning from mistakes.
Compromise	1	When goals are important, but not worth the effort or potential disruption of more assertive modes.
	2	When opponents with equal power are committed to mutually exclusive goals.
	3	To achieve temporary settlements to complex issues.
	4	To arrive at expedient solutions under time pressure.
	5	As a backup when collaboration or competition is unsuccessful.

Figure 11.2 Use of the five conflict handling orientations
Source: Thomas 1977

or orientation. There will be situations when quick decisive action is needed against other people who will take advantage of anything other than a competitive stance, leaving you no option but to force the issue. Figure 11.2 outlines the other aspects of conflict management in more detail.

REFLECTION (1)

Consider aspects of conflict in which you have been involved and the action taken. Which of the five approaches were used?

Despite the guidelines on conflict handling every manager needs to judge the degree of turbulence which is acceptable within the workplace and its effect on staff performance. Rosenfield's (1995) diagram (Figure 11.3) is a useful starting-point but the absence of any quantitative measures necessarily limits interpretation and subsequent value.

For this reason, Kanter's (1990) signals of destructive competition are more useful. She sees signals of destructive competition as:

1   More attention is paid to beating rivals than to performing tasks well.
2   Friendly competition between people who respect one another is replaced by mistrust, suspicion and scorn.
3   Imitation may drive out innovation.
4   The weaker party may give up rather than continue to fight.
5   When that happens, the stronger party begins to feel dangerously invincible.

In the case study it is clear that unless there is conflict resolution the outcomes described by Kanter could push staff into a 'winners and losers' situation where either member of staff may seek support from other team members.

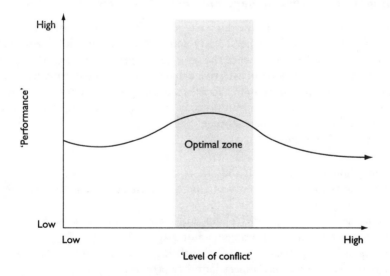

Figure 11.3 The effect of conflict on organisational performance

These views are supported by Schein (1980) in his chapter on the negative effects of inter-group competition when he says:

> 'Win–lose' situations should be avoided and groups (or individuals) should never be put into the position of competing for some scarce organizational reward: emphasis should always be placed on pooling resources to maximize organizational effectiveness, rewards should be shared equally with all groups or departments.
>
> (Schein 1980: 180)

Methods of coping with conflict

Because of the competitive nature of conflict one party will always feel demeaned and suspicious and will often try to leave for another post. Others may adopt the following strategies adapted from Argyris (1973):

1   Defence reactions, a lessening of interest and general slowing down.
2   Working within an informal group network to support ideas and self esteem.
3   Viewing work from a more material and detached standpoint that accepts less personal development.
4   Working with new staff to develop a culture that embraces your views.
5   Becoming more assertive through speech expression, eye contact and action.

Coping with conflict by becoming more assertive

Within any school or centre the degree of sensitivity to conflict will naturally depend upon an individual's personality and communication skills. Although they may be powerless to influence the structural aspects of conflict, the opportunity to increase their level of assertive behaviour nevertheless remains. A satisfactory conclusion to the conflict in the case study would be for both staff to become more assertive by communicating openly their anxieties about work and their feelings towards one another.

Being assertive means:

- being honest with yourself and others;
- being able to say what you want, need or feel, but not at the expense of other people;
- being self-confident, positive and understanding other people's points of view and behaving in a rational, adult way;
- being able to negotiate and reach workable compromises;
- having self-respect and respect for other people.

In communication terms it requires you to:

Step 1   Actively listen to what is being said, then show the other person that you both hear and understand them.
Step 2   Say what you think and what you feel.
Step 3   Say what you want to happen.

An analysis of Marilyn's behaviour in the case study would show that she is unable to follow step 2 – since she is unable to communicate her thoughts honestly.

REFLECTION (2)

How can the manager help her staff to become more assertive?

Managing stress

Many of the causes of stress are to be found in the earlier pages, and indeed the preceding chapters. Enough has been written and independent data produced to convince the most sceptical observer that teachers and all those working in education settings now rate very highly in the stress leagues, as measured by the *Sunday Times* Occupational Stress Register (1997) and other agencies.

The nature of stress

It is not our intention to detail the nature of stress; suffice it to say that, up to a point, some stress is useful while too much stress is harmful. The case study clearly illustrates how staff may become stressed by situations which emphasise their lack of power and control. Uncertainty and the prospect of change play a significant part in creating conflict and stress. Changes, such as the introduction of Nursery Inspections, Baseline Assessment and Desirable Learning Outcomes in under-fives settings may result in feelings of stress for early years workers, as did similar experiences in schools, following the introduction of the National Curriculum, performance tables and Ofsted inspections.

Although the causes of stress are well known and easy to identify (see page 172) there still appears to be a reluctance on the part of many managers to acknowledge stress-related behaviour as anything more than a slightly deteriorating behaviour pattern.

Our experience of running one-day courses on stress management has been to begin by asking staff to write down what causes them stress in their work and what they feel the school or centre could do to reduce such harmful pressures.

Causes of stress identified in stress management courses and staff supervision

- Heavy workloads, government legislation including inspection and performance tables.
- Parental pressure, changes in attitude, pupil indiscipline and motivation.
- Poor management and organisation, including communication, increased bureaucracy.
- Low morale, poor pay and status.
- Lack of staff development and poor career prospects.
- Cuts in spending, insecurity of temporary contracts and reduced opportunities for early retirement.
- Rigid rotas; shortage of staff; maintaining Children's Act ratios at all times; staff absences.

Two significant findings emerge. First, everyone should be encouraged to keep a personal record or log and from that develop an action plan. Second, a school or centre audit should be undertaken by a working party to examine hazards and provide evidence of worrying trends. Such action, supported by managers, heads and governors should underline their organisational commitment to what can rapidly develop into an enormous psychological burden of escalating cost.

These suggestions, adapted from Brown (1993), remain some of the best advice for dealing with stress at an organisational level:

- The development of staff support groups.
- Training a staff member as a counsellor.
- Seeking help through the Local Authority.
- The development of networks between schools/centres.
- The use of in-service days to develop action plans to alleviate staff stress at every level.
- Encouraging staff to use the system of appraisal as a means of identifying such training needs as will enable them to reduce their stress.
- Looking at overall communication networks and processes.
- Conducting a stress audit and developing ways of responding to identified concerns.
- Assessing the establishment's meetings policy.

Further reading

We have selected two books that will help you develop conflict management skills and one concerned with stress management. The first is **Improve Your People Skills** (1988) Peter Honey. The book is more of a guide in that it adopts an alphabetical format that begins with Action Plans and ends with

ACTIVITY

Finally the problem begins (and ends) with individuals, and so it is worthwhile looking at the following nineteen-point plan (Figure 11.4) as the basis for an action plan. Begin by taking a fresh look at yourself and finally learn to accept what you can't change.

1	Know yourself.
2	Cultivate your sense of humour.
3	Be active and productive.
4	Keep things in perspective.
5	Don't dwell on or worry about problems.
6	Have a variety of interests.
7	Have a variety of responses to situations.
8	Accept others' values.
9	Talk to someone (anyone) about your problems.
10	Relax after and forget work at the end of the day.
11	Organise 'free' time for yourself.
12	Avoid confrontations, avoid getting angry.
13	Set priorities.
14	Think of good things in the future.
15	Try and get away for a break when you can.
16	Look after yourself physically and mentally.
17	Be realistic in your goals.
18	Deal with your anger.
19	Learn to accept what you can't change.

Figure 11.4 Nineteen coping strategies for life

Worry. While there are clear advantages in terms of looking up a reference the drawback is that many of the entries are rather too short. Nevertheless, the entry on conflict distinguishes well between facing it aggressively or assertively:

Facing conflict aggressively means:

- Being secretive about your real objective.
- Exaggerating your case.
- Refusing to concede that the other person has a valid point.
- Belittling the other person's points.
- Repeating your case dogmatically.
- Disagreeing.
- Interrupting the other person.

Facing conflict assertively means:

- Being open about your objective.
- Establishing what the other person's objective is.
- Searching for common ground.
- Stating your case clearly.
- Understanding the other person's case.

(Honey 1988: 36)

Equally valuable is the section on assertiveness, 'a collection of behaviours that stem from a belief that your needs or wants are as important as other people's'. Guidelines on 'helpful behaviour' provide another valuable checklist worth circulating to all workers:

- Lean forward with hands open, arms uncrossed and legs uncrossed.
- Look at the other person for approximately 60 per cent of the time.
- When listening, nod and make 'I'm listening' noises such as 'um', 'yes', 'really'.
- Smile.
- Sit beside the other person or if this isn't possible, at a 90 degree angle to them.
- Use the other person's name early on in the transaction.
- Ask the other person open questions.
- Summarize back to the other person what you think they have said.
- Say things that refer back to what the other person has said.
- Show empathy by saying you understand how the other person feels and can see things from their point of view.
- When in agreement with the other person, openly say so and say why.
- Build on the other person's ideas.
- Be non-judgmental towards the other person.
- If you have to disagree with the other person, give the reason first then say you disagree.
- Admit it when you don't know the answer or have made a mistake.
- Openly explain what you are doing, or intending to do, for the other person.
- Be genuine, with visual and verbal behaviours telling the same story.

(Honey 1988: 84)

Finally, sections on negotiating and persuasiveness ensure that time spent reading just a few sections could save hours of fruitless activity and hindrance.

Our second book is *Leadership Skills For Women* (1989) **Marilyn Manning and Patricia Haddock**. This is a popular text that recognises the part that 'gender specific behaviour' plays in leadership style. It begins by considering the characteristics of effective leaders through different styles, identifying the supporter and the perfectionist as quiet leadership styles, with the director and motivator as outgoing ones. Interspersed are exercises, self analysis and quotations, many of which get to the heart of the issue: 'Your attitude speaks so loudly, employees can't hear what you say' (p. 15), and 'Example is not the main thing in influencing others, it is the only thing' (p. 25).

Chapters on teams, planning tools and personal power are all useful supplements to any manager's skills and chapter 4, 'Leaders are problem solvers', contains valuable advice on conflict resolution, with exercises and examples of seven difficult personality types.

Seven difficult personality types

1   **Attackers**
    Behaviour: Attackers assert their viewpoint forcefully. They require people to listen to what they say. They need room and time to blow off steam.
    Your action: Address the attacker by name and quietly, but firmly, ask her or him to sit. Then listen carefully to what the attacker has to say. Once calmed, the attacker usually becomes reasonable and may suggest valuable solutions. The worst coping behaviour on your part would be to return the attack.

2   **Egotists**
    Behaviour: Egotists also assert themselves but, unlike attackers, they may be subject experts.
    Your action: Show honest respect for their knowledge, but don't become intimidated by it. Instead, capitalise on what they know by asking questions. Compliment them when they provide helpful information but make sure they know you are the leader.

3   **Sneaks**
    Behaviour: Sneaks take 'potshots' and often use sarcasm as a weapon.
    Your action: Confront sneaks with direct questions and let them know you do not appreciate their sarcasm. Use positive reinforcement when possible to steer them towards becoming more of a team player.

4   **Victims**
    Behaviour: Victims see everything negatively. They appear powerless and defeated, often whining about everyone and everything.
    Your action: Ask them for suggestions to improve the situation. Have them state the negatives and address each logically and positively.

5   **Negators**
    Behaviour: Negators are usually suspicious of those in authority and believe that their way of doing things is the only way.
    Your action: Let negators use their negative 'ammunition' in a group meeting, then let colleagues express their views about possible

solutions. They will usually try to 'enlighten' negators that better solutions exist.

6 **Super-agreeable people**
Behaviour: Super-agreeable people have such a strong need to be liked that they will do whatever you request at the expense of their own needs. They will overcommit and often disappoint and frustrate everyone.
Your action: Monitor assignments to make sure they are not over-worked.

7 **Unresponsive people**
Behaviour: Unresponsive people are the most difficult people to manage. They are seemingly impossible to draw out.
Your action: Use open-ended questions that require more than a 'Yes' or 'No' answer. Wait for a response. Resist the urge to finish sentences for them. Follow up on actions assigned to them and give them assignments to present at future meetings.

(Manning and Haddock 1989: 50–2)

Coaching and counselling is addressed briefly through self-rating questions and a section on the value of feedback.

Despite being limited in its theory this is a useful short text designed to give managers greater confidence in areas of challenge or aspects of potential stress.

Stress Management **(1982) Edward Charlesworth and Ronald Nathan** is subtitled 'a comprehensive guide to wellness' and comprises eight sections that begin with learning about stress and life in 'the twentieth century, the age of anxiety'. It goes on to distinguish between physical and emotional stress, resistance and disease and finally healthy stress. A chapter on beginning to manage your stress follows, suggesting relaxation and professional help. The succeeding chapters provide a wide range of practical suggestions designed to reduce tension by scanning one's body and adopting structured breathing exercises. Muscle relaxation is detailed, along with countdown techniques designed to provide greater feelings of well being. 'Imagery training, the windows of your mind' provides a range of suggestions designed to counteract upsetting thoughts and allow people to focus on more relaxing themes.

Life-change management through the social readjustment rating scale is another useful focus that when combined with The Type A/B Lifestyle Questionnaire in Figure 11.5 allows the reader to form a clearer picture of their work and personal situation.

The Type A/B Lifestyle Questionnaire

Directions

As you can see, each scale in the Questionnaire is composed of a pair of adjectives or phrases. Each pair represents two kinds of contrasting behaviour. Choose the number that most closely represents the type of person you are and put it under the column labelled 'Your score'. Add your scores to get your total score.

What your total A/B score means

If your total score is 160–200, and especially if you are over 40 and smoke, you may have a high risk of developing cardiac illness.

If your total score is 100–134, you are a mixture of A and B patterns. Beware of any potential for slipping into A behaviour.

If your total score is less than 100, your behaviour is generally relaxed and you express few of the reactions associated with cardiac disease. You probably have a Type B pattern.

Your score should give you some idea of where you stand in the discussion

---

RATING SCALE

				Your score
1	Work regular hours	0 1 2 3 4 5 6 7 8 9 10	Bring work home or work late	____
2	Wait calmly	0 1 2 3 4 5 6 7 8 9 10	Wait impatiently	____
3	Seldom judge in terms of numbers (How many, how much)	0 1 2 3 4 5 6 7 8 9 10	Place value in terms of numbers	____
4	Not competitive	0 1 2 3 4 5 6 7 8 9 10	Very competitive	____
5	Feel limited responsibility	0 1 2 3 4 5 6 7 8 9 10	Always feel responsible	____
6	Unhurried about appointments	0 1 2 3 4 5 6 7 8 9 10	Frequently hurried for appointments	____
7	Never in a hurry	0 1 2 3 4 5 6 7 8 9 10	Always in a hurry	____
8	Many interests	0 1 2 3 4 5 6 7 8 9 10	Work is main interest	____
9	Try to satisfy self	0 1 2 3 4 5 6 7 8 9 10	Want to be recognised by others	____
10	Not very precise	0 1 2 3 4 5 6 7 8 9 10	Careful about detail	____
11	Can leave things temporarily unfinished	0 1 2 3 4 5 6 7 8 9 10	Must get things finished	____
12	Satisfied with job	0 1 2 3 4 5 6 7 8 9 10	Striving on the job	____
13	Listen well	0 1 2 3 4 5 6 7 8 9 10	Finish sentences for others	____
14	Easygoing	0 1 2 3 4 5 6 7 8 9 10	Hard driving	____
15	Do things slowly	0 1 2 3 4 5 6 7 8 9 10	Do things quickly	____
16	Do one thing at a time	0 1 2 3 4 5 6 7 8 9 10	Think about what to do next	____
17	Rarely angry	0 1 2 3 4 5 6 7 8 9 10	Easily angered	____
18	Slow speech	0 1 2 3 4 5 6 7 8 9 10	Forceful speech	____
19	Express feelings easily	0 1 2 3 4 5 6 7 8 9 10	Bottle up feelings	____
20	Rarely set deadlines	0 1 2 3 4 5 6 7 8 9 10	Often set deadlines	____

YOUR TOTAL A/B SCORE   ____

Figure 11.5 The Type A/B Lifestyle Questionnaire
Source: Charlesworth and Nathan 1982

of Type A behaviour. Even Type B persons occasionally slip into Type A behaviour. It is important to remember that any of these patterns can change over time.

The final chapter in this section considers approaches to handling anxiety through positive talking, concentrating on effective self talk when anxious moments arise. This is developed through a detailed consideration of anger management and assertiveness, using a framework of communication styles and role play to give guidelines for successful outcomes.

Maintaining one's physical health and mental well being rounds off the book, with guidance on diet and exercise as well as a section on positive self-control that contains Waitley's ten characteristics of people who appear to succeed in managing stress and living satisfying lives.

His ten qualities of a winner include:

1 Positive self-awareness: understanding where you are coming from.
2 Positive self-esteem: liking yourself.
3 Positive self-control: making it happen for yourself.
4 Positive self-motivation: wanting to and deciding you can.
5 Positive self-expectancy: deciding that next time you will do even better.
6 Positive self-image: seeing yourself changing and growing.
7 Positive self-direction: having a game plan.
8 Positive self-discipline: practising mentally.
9 Positive self-dimension: valuing yourself as a person.
10 Positive self-projection: reflecting yourself in how you walk, talk, and listen.

(Waitley 1978)

We can think of no better way to conclude.

References

Chapter I

Bryman, A. (1986) *Charisma and Leadership in Organizations*, Sage.

Fayol, H. (1987) *General and Industrial Management*, Pitman.

Fielder, F. (1967) *A Theory of Leadership Effectiveness*, McGraw Hill.

Hickman, C. and Silva, M. (1988) *Creating Excellence*, Unwin.

Luthans, F., Hodgetts, R.M. and Rosenkrantz, S. (1988) *Real Managers*, Ballinger.

Shea, M. (1993) *Personal Impact, Presence, Para-language and the Art of Good Communication*, Sinclair.

Stogdill, R. (1974) *Handbook of Leadership*, Free Press.

Yukl, G. (1989) *Leadership in Organizations*, Prentice Hall.

Chapter 2

Baron, R. (1986) (2nd edn) *Behaviour in Organizations*, Allyn and Bacon.

Benne, K.D. and Sheats, P. (1948) 'Effective and Ineffective Behaviour in Groups: Functional Roles of Group Members', *Journal of Social Issues*, Spring: 41–9.

Kakabadse, A., Ludlow, R. and Vinnicombe, S. (1988) *Working in Organizations*, Penguin.

Luthans, F. (1985) (4th edn) *Organizational Behaviour,* McGraw Hill.

Zajonc, R. (1980) 'Comprescence' in P.B. Paulus (ed.) *Psychology of Group Influence*, Erlbaum.

Chapter 3

Dyer, W. (1987) (2nd edn) *Team Building*, Addison Wesley.

Gillen, T. (1997) *Positive Influencing Skills*, IPD.

Thibaut, J., Spence, J. and Carson, R. (eds) *Contemporary Topics in Social Psychology*, General Learning.

Williams, H. (1996) *Managing Groups and Teams*, Prentice Hall.

Chapter 4

Deming, W.E. (1986) *Out of the Crisis*, Cambridge University Press.

Drucker, P. (1990) *Management*, Pan.

Greenwood, M. and Gaunt, H. (1994) *Total Quality Management for Schools*, Cassell.

Herzberg, F. (1966) 'The Motivation–Hygiene Theory' in V. Vroom and E. Deci (eds) *Management and Motivation*, Penguin.

Martin, P. and Nicholls, J. (1987) *Creating Workforce*, Institute of Personal Management.

Neave, H. (1990) *The Deming Dimension*, SPC Press.

Steers, R. and Porter, L. (1983) (3rd edn) *Motivation and Work Behaviour*, McGraw Hill.

Vroom, V. and Deci, E. (eds) (1970) *Management and Motivation*, Penguin.

Chapter 5

Burke, W. (1978) *Cutting Edge: Current Theory and Practice in Organizational Development*, University associates United States.

Dalin, P. and Rust, V. (1983) *Can Schools Learn*, NFER-NELSON.

Havelock, R. (1973) *The Change Agent's Guide to Innovation in Education*, Educational Technology Publications.

Kotter, J., Schlesinger, L. and Sathe, V. (eds) (1986) *Organization: Text, Cases and Readings on the Management of Organizational Design and Change*, Irwin.

Leigh, A. (1994) *Effective Change*, IPM.

Owens, R. (1987) (3rd edn) *Organizational Behaviour in Education*, Prentice Hall.

Pedler, M., Burgoyne, J. and Boydell, T. (1978) *A Manager's Guide to Self Development*, McGraw Hill.

Watson, L. (1986) 'The Loser and the Management of Change', *School Organization*, vol. 6, no.1.

Wilson, D. (1992) *A Strategy of Change*, Routledge.

Chapter 6

Bell, L. (1988) *Management Skills for Primary Schools*, Routledge.

Drucker, P. (1979) *Management*, Pan.

Everard, B. and Morris, G. (1990) (2nd edn) *Effective School Management*, Paul Chapman Publishing.

Feldman, D. and Arnold, H. (1985) *Managing Individuals and Group Behaviour in Organisations*, McGraw Hill.

Gilmore, S. and Fraleigh, P. (1993) *Communication at Work*, Friendly Press.

Leigh, A. (1994) *Effective Change*, IPM.

Myers, M. and Myers, G. (1982) *Managing by Communication*, McGraw Hill.

Peel, M. (1990) *Improving Your Communication Skills*, Kogan Page.

Pinker. S. (1995) *Language Instinct*, Penguin.

Trethowan, D. (1986) *Communication in Schools*, Industrial Society.

Chapter 7

Day, C., Johnston, D. and Whitaker, P. (1985) *Managing Primary Schools*, Harper Row.

Drucker, P. (1977) *Management*, Pan.

Grout, J. (1995) 'Exit interviews', in *Management Today*, January.

Hilton, R.H. (1986) Unpublished lecture notes, Edge Hill University College.

Owens, R. (1987) (3rd edn) *Organizational Behaviour in Education*, Prentice Hall.
Seifert, R. (1996) *Human Resource Management in Schools*, Pitman Publishing.
Shackleton, V.W. (1989) *How to Pick People for Jobs*, Fontana.
Southworth, G. (1990) *Staff Selection in the Primary School*, Blackwell Education.
Trice, H. and Beyer, J. (1984) *The Cultures of Work Organizations*, Prentice Hall.

Chapter 8

Gratus, J. (1988) *Successful Interviewing: How to Find and Keep the Best People*, Penguin (Business).

Chapter 9

Day, C., Whitaker, P. and Johnston, D. (1990) *Managing Primary Schools*, Paul Chapman.
Francis, D. and Woodcock, M. (1982) *50 activities for self-development*, Gower Publishing Company.
Gilmore, S. and Fraleigh, P. (1993) *Communication at Work*, Friendly Press.
Hands, G. (1981) 'First catch your adviser: the INSET role of advisers', in C. Donoughue *et al. In-service, the Teacher and the School*, Kogan Page.
Handy, C. (1994) *The Empty Raincoat*, Arrow Books.
Hoare, D. (1987) 'Succeeding by self-audit', in *Management Today*, April.
Joyce, B. and Showers, B. (1980) 'Improving in-service training: the message to research', *Educational Leadership*, February: 379–85.
Kanter, R.M. (1990) *The Change Masters*, Unwin.
Kemp, J.E. (1981) *Staff Development in Schools*, Sheffield City Polytechnic.
Morant, R. (1981) *In-service Education Within the School*, Unwin.
O'Sullivan, F., Jones, K. and Reid, K. (1988) S*taff Development in the Secondary School*, Hodder and Stoughton.

Chapter 10

Davies, B. and Ellison, L. (1991) *Developing a Marketing Culture in a School*, Longman.
Dennison, W. (1989) 'The competitive edge', in *School Organization*, vol. 9, no. 2.
Greenhall, J. (1987) *Public Relations Management*, HEIST publications.
Kotler, P. and Fox, K. (1985) *Strategic Marketing for Educational Institutions*, Prentice Hall.
Margerson, C. (1988) *Management Consulting Skills*, Gower.

Chapter 11

Argyris, C. (1973) (2nd edn) *Organization and Innovation*, Irwin.
Brown, M. (1993) *Managing Schools Today*, no. 5.
Charlesworth, E. and Nathan, R. (1982) *Stress Management: A Comprehensive Guide to Wellness*, Souvenir Press.
Honey, P. (1988) *Improve Your People Skills*, IPM.
Kanter, R.M. (1990) *When Giants Learn to Dance*, Unwin.

Lippitt, G. (1983) 'Managing conflict in today's organisations', in G. Lippitt and B. Taylor (eds) *Management Development and Training Handbook*, McGraw Hill.

Luthans, F. (1985) (4th edn) *Organizational Behaviour*, McGraw Hill.

Manning, M. and Haddock, P. (1989) *Leadership Skills for Women*, Kogan Page.

Mullins, L. (1989) (2nd edn) *Management and Organisational Behaviour*, Pitman.

Owens, R. (1987) *Organizational Behaviour in Education*, Prentice Hall.

Robbins, S. (1989) (4th edn) *Organizational Behaviour*, Prentice Hall.

Rosenfield, P. (1995) *Impression Management in Organizations*, Routledge.

Schein, E. (1980) (3rd edn) *Organizational Psychology*, Prentice Hall.

Thomas, K. (1977) 'Conflict and Conflict Management', in M. Dunnett (ed.) *Handbook of Industrial and Organizational Psychology*, Rand McNally.

Waitley, D. (1978) *The Psychology of Winning*, Nightingale.

Index